FANTASTIC FACTS

Miles Kelly

First published in 2022 by Miles Kelly Publishing Ltd
Harding's Barn, Bardfield End Green, Thaxted, Essex, CM6 3PX, UK
Unit 5A The Court, Ashbourne Industrial Estate, Ashbourne,
Co. Meath, A84 DP73, Eire

Copyright © Miles Kelly Publishing Ltd 2022

4 6 8 10 12 11 9 7 5

Publishing Director Belinda Gallagher
Creative Director Jo Cowan
Editorial Director Rosie Neave
Senior Editor Amy Johnson
Senior Designer Emily Stalley
Image Manager Liberty Newton
Indexer Michelle Baker
Production Elizabeth Collins
Reprographics Stephan Davis
Assets Venita Kidwai

All rights reserved. No part of this publication may be reproduced, stored in a retrieval system, or transmitted by any means, electronic, mechanical, photocopying, recording or otherwise, without the prior permission of the copyright holder.

ISBN 978-1-78989-528-5

Printed in China

British Library Cataloguing-in-Publication Data
A catalogue record for this book is available from the British Library

Made with paper from a sustainable forest

www.mileskelly.net

CONTENTS

EARTH AND SPACE 4

 SCIENCE 44

DINOSAURS 84

 ANIMALS 96

ANCIENT HISTORY 116

 INDEX 156

ACKNOWLEDGEMENTS 159

EARTH AND SPACE

1 Space is all around Earth! It officiallly begins 100 kilometres up from sea level, above our atmosphere (the layer of gases that surrounds the planet). Space contains many exciting things such as planets, moons, stars and galaxies. Gas and dust fill the huge spaces between them.

2 Distances in space are vast — so huge that astronomers do not use kilometres or miles to measure them. One measure of distance is the light-year, which is the distance that light travels in one year, and is equal to 9.46 million million kilometres. The nearest star to the Sun is 4.2 light-years away — equivalent to nearly 40 million million kilometres.

▶ Astronauts wear spacesuits to go outside a space station or a spacecraft. Spacesuits supply astronauts with air and water and protect them from speeding dust and harmful radiation.

3 **People who travel in space are called astronauts.** The furthest humans have ever been is to the Moon, around 384,400 kilometres away. The journey to get there took three days. Since 2000, there have been astronauts living and working on the International Space Station, which circles Earth about 350 kilometres above sea level.

Our life-giving star

4 **The Sun is our nearest star.** Most stars are so far away they look like points of light in the sky, but the Sun looks different because it is much closer to us. The Sun is not solid, like Earth. It is a huge ball of super-hot gases, so hot that they glow like the flames of a bonfire.

◄ The Sun's hot, glowing gas is always on the move, bubbling up to the surface and sinking back down again.

5 **Nothing could live on Earth without the Sun.** Deep in its centre the Sun is constantly making energy that keeps its gases hot and glowing. This energy works its way to the surface where it escapes as heat and light. Without it, Earth would be cold and dark with no life at all.

PROMINENCE

Solar prominences can reach temperatures of 10,000°C.

SOLAR FLARE

Solar flares erupt in a few minutes, then take more than half an hour to die away again.

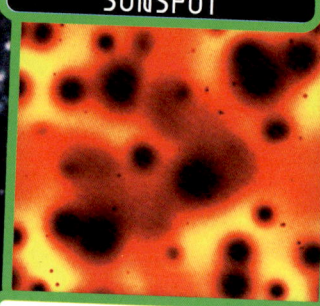

SUNSPOT

Groups of sunspots seem to move across the Sun over two weeks, as the Sun rotates.

EARTH AND SPACE

6 **The Sun is often spotty.** Sunspots appear on the surface, some wider than Earth. They look dark because they are cooler than the rest of the Sun. Solar flares – explosions of energy – can suddenly shoot out from the Sun. The Sun also throws huge loops of gas called prominences out into space.

▼ When the Moon casts a shadow on Earth, there is a solar eclipse.

Sun

Moon

Earth

Solar eclipse

7 **When the Moon hides the Sun there is a solar eclipse.** Every so often, the Sun, Moon and Earth line up in space so that the Moon comes directly between the Earth and the Sun. This stops the sunlight from reaching a small area on Earth. This area grows dark and cold, as if night has come early.

▲ A photo of a solar eclipse on 1 August 2008 shows the Moon totally blocking the Sun, and reveals the Sun's halo-like corona – part of its atmosphere not normally seen because the Sun's surface is too bright.

I DON'T BELIEVE IT!
The surface of the Sun is nearly 60 times hotter than boiling water. It is so hot it would melt a spacecraft flying near it.

WARNING
Never look directly at the Sun, especially not through a telescope or binoculars. It is so bright it will harm your eyes and could even make you blind.

A family of planets

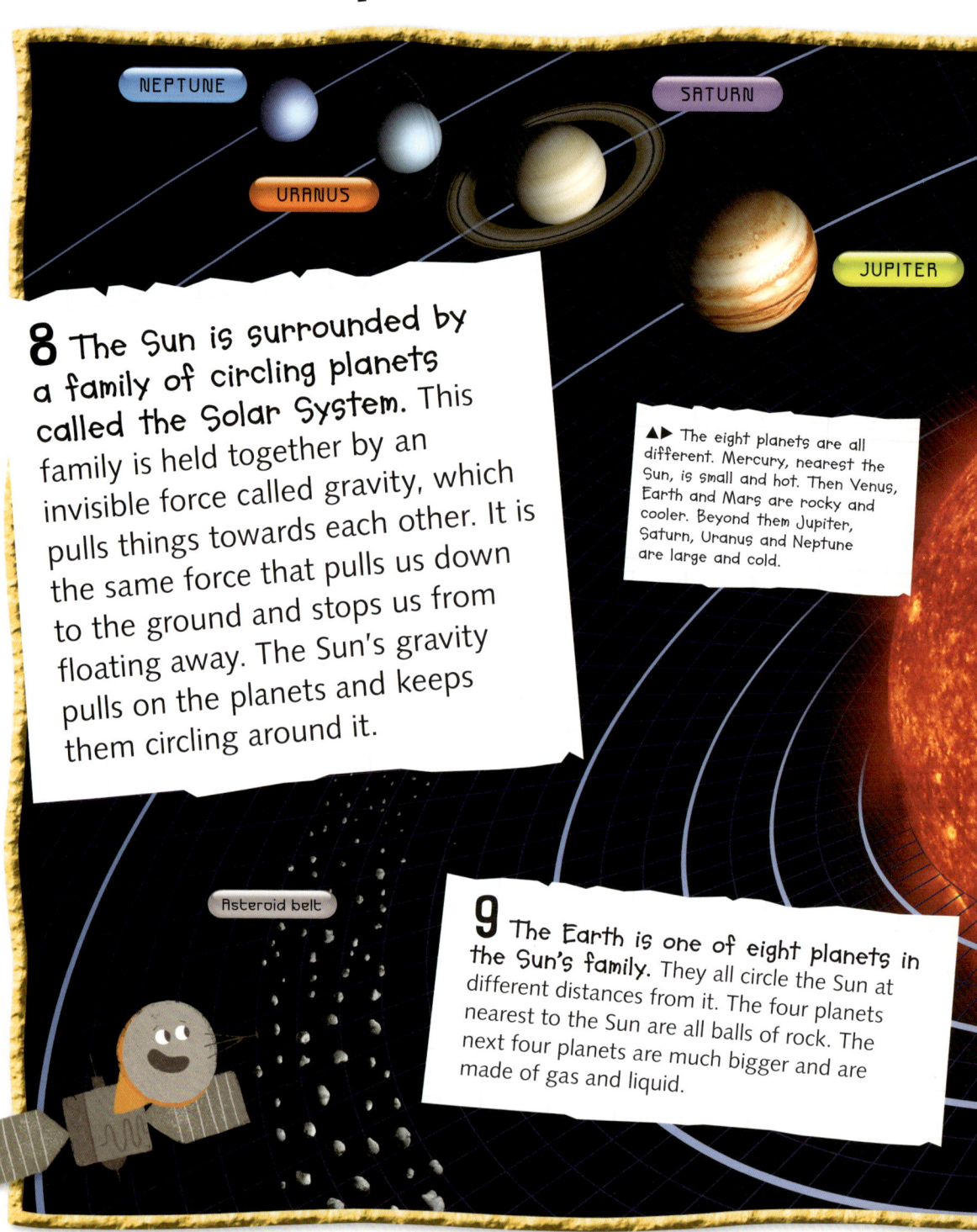

8 The Sun is surrounded by a family of circling planets called the Solar System. This family is held together by an invisible force called gravity, which pulls things towards each other. It is the same force that pulls us down to the ground and stops us from floating away. The Sun's gravity pulls on the planets and keeps them circling around it.

▲▶ The eight planets are all different. Mercury, nearest the Sun, is small and hot. Then Venus, Earth and Mars are rocky and cooler. Beyond them Jupiter, Saturn, Uranus and Neptune are large and cold.

9 The Earth is one of eight planets in the Sun's family. They all circle the Sun at different distances from it. The four planets nearest to the Sun are all balls of rock. The next four planets are much bigger and are made of gas and liquid.

EARTH AND SPACE

10 **Moons circle the planets, travelling with them round the Sun.** Earth has one moon. It circles the Earth while the Earth circles round the Sun. Mars has two tiny moons, but Mercury and Venus have none at all. There are large families of moons, like miniature solar systems, around all the large gas planets.

I DON'T BELIEVE IT!

If the Sun was the size of a large beach ball, the Earth would be as small as a pea, and the Moon would look like a pinhead.

SUN
MARS
Earth's Moon
EARTH
VENUS
MERCURY

11 **There are millions of smaller members in the Sun's family.** Some are tiny specks of dust speeding through space between the planets. Larger chunks of rock, many as large as mountains, are called asteroids. Comets come from the edge of the Solar System, skimming past the Sun before they disappear again.

Billions of galaxies

12 **The Sun is part of a huge family of stars called the Milky Way Galaxy.** There are billions of other stars in our galaxy, as many as the grains of sand on a beach. We call it the Milky Way because it looks like a very faint band of light in the night sky, as though someone has spilt some milk across space.

▼ With binoculars you can see that the faint glow of the Milky Way comes from millions of stars in our galaxy.

13 **Curling arms give some galaxies their spiral shape.** The Milky Way has arms made of bright stars and glowing clouds of gas that curl round into a spiral shape. Some galaxies, called elliptical galaxies, have a round shape like a squashed ball. Other galaxies have no particular shape.

I DON'T BELIEVE IT!
If you could fit the Milky Way onto these two pages, the Sun would be so tiny, you could not see it.

EARTH AND SPACE

A CLUSTER OF GALAXIES

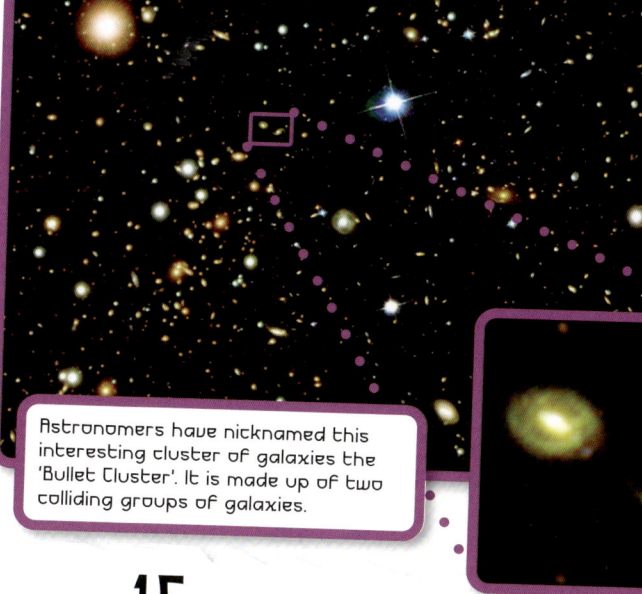

Astronomers have nicknamed this interesting cluster of galaxies the 'Bullet Cluster'. It is made up of two colliding groups of galaxies.

14 There are billions of galaxies outside the Milky Way. Some are larger than the Milky Way and many are smaller, but they all have more stars than you can count. The galaxies tend to stay together in groups called clusters.

▲ Galaxies can be categorized by their shape. The Milky Way is a spiral galaxy.

15 There is no bump when galaxies collide. A galaxy is mostly empty space between the stars. But when galaxies get very close they can pull each other out of shape. Sometimes they look as if they have grown a huge tail stretching out into space, or their shape may change into a ring of glowing stars.

▲ These two galaxies are so close that each has pulled a long tail of bright stars from the other.

Where did Earth come from?

16 Scientists think Earth formed from a huge cloud of gas and dust around 4500 million years ago. A massive explosion of a star – a supernova – caused the cloud to collapse in on itself. It formed a spinning disc and grew bigger. Gases gathered at its centre, forming the Sun. Dust whizzed around the Sun and clumped together into lumps of rock. In time the rocks collided, forming the planets.

❸ A clump grows large enough that its pull of gravity shapes it into a planet

❷ As the clumps grew bigger their gravity pulled more dust and rock towards them

❶ Dust and rock in the spinning disc clumped together

❹ The early Earth continues to grow and is bombarded with meteorites

❻ Land on Earth was once one supercontinent that continually broke apart and smashed back together. It is now split into seven continents

❺ Volcanoes erupt, releasing gases, helping to form the early atmosphere

17 **The early Earth was extremely hot.** It might have been made almost completely of molten rock. Over hundreds of millions of years the Earth cooled and layers formed. Liquid rock sank towards the centre, leaving a thin solid shell, or crust, at the surface.

▲ Like the other Solar System planets, Earth formed from small pieces of rock and dust that collided with each other, gradually forming larger and larger objects.

EARTH AND SPACE

18 Huge numbers of large rocks called meteorites crashed into the Earth. They made round hollows called craters on the surface. The Moon was hit with meteorites at the same time. Look at the Moon with binoculars – you can see the craters that were made long ago.

▶ The Moon has huge craters, and mountain ranges up to 5000 metres high. As the Moon doesn't have wind or flowing water, there is nothing to fill in the craters.

▶ Erupting volcanoes and fierce storms helped form the atmosphere and oceans. These provided energy that was needed for life on Earth to begin.

19 The oceans and seas formed as the Earth cooled down. Volcanoes erupted, letting out steam, gases and rocks from inside the Earth. As the Earth cooled, the steam changed to water droplets and made clouds. As the Earth cooled further, rain fell from the clouds. It rained for millions of years to make the seas and oceans.

I DON'T BELIEVE IT!
Millions of rocks enter Earth's atmosphere as it speeds through space. Some larger ones may reach the ground as meteorites.

Our home in space

20 **Earth is the third planet from the Sun.** It is the only place in the Universe known to have liquid water and the ability to support life. It takes 24 hours to spin once, giving us night and day, and 365 days (a year) to orbit the Sun.

21 **One of the rocky planets, Earth consists of several layers.** The thin crust of rock that forms its surface sits on top of a deeper layer of rock called the mantle. Below the mantle, in the middle of the planet, there is a solid iron core with liquid iron around it.

22 **Earth's atmosphere is a mixture of gases, mainly nitrogen and oxygen.** It also contains some water vapour, carbon dioxide and tiny traces of other gases. This mixture of gases is called air, and it makes life on Earth possible.

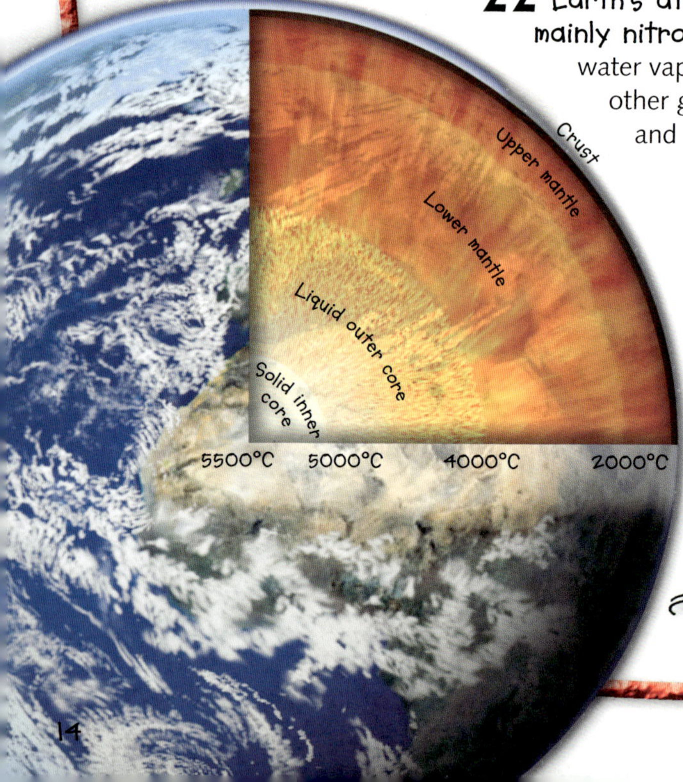

► Life on Earth began in the oceans about 3.8 billion years ago and then spread across the whole planet.

◄ Earth's core is as hot as the surface of the Sun.

Crust
Upper mantle
Lower mantle
Liquid outer core
Solid inner core
5500°C 5000°C 4000°C 2000°C

I DON'T BELIEVE IT!
A day on Earth is 24 hours long today, but billions of years ago Earth was spinning much faster. A day was only 14 hours long. Earth's spin has been slowing down ever since.

▼ The weather changes from one season to the next because of Earth's tilt.

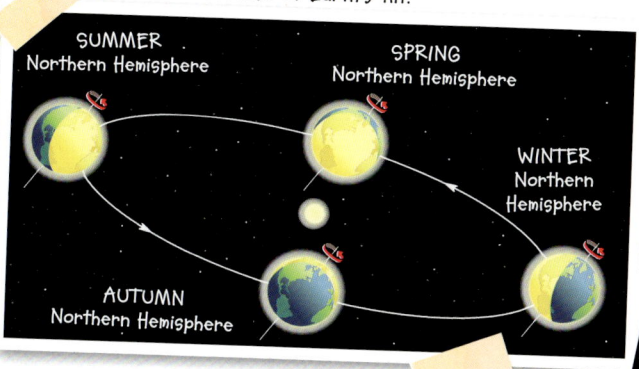

▼ Earth's magnetic field extends far out into space. It protects us from the 'solar wind' — charged particles streaming out of the Sun.

23 **Earth tilts as it travels around the Sun, like a spinning top leaning over.** This tilt produces the seasons. When the North Pole tilts towards the Sun, the northern half of Earth is warmer and the southern half is colder. As Earth moves around the Sun, the North Pole tilts away from the Sun. The northern half of Earth cools and the southern half warms up.

24 **Earth behaves like a giant magnet with a north pole and a south pole.** Liquid iron swirling around in Earth's core creates electrical currents that produce its magnetic field.

25 **Particles flying out of the Sun cause an eerie glow in the sky called an aurora.** Earth's magnetic field steers the particles into the upper atmosphere near the North and South poles. Here they collide with particles of gas, making them glow.

Fact file: EARTH

Named after: An old English word for the ground or soil
Diameter: 12,756 kilometres
Distance from the Sun: 149.6 million kilometres
Time to spin once: 23.9 hours
Time to orbit the Sun: 365.2 days
Average temperature: 15°C
Number of moons: 1

◀ Auroras light up the sky near the poles, seen from the International Space Station (left). They are known as the Northern Lights (*Aurora Borealis*) and Southern Lights (*Aurora Australis*).

massive mountains

26 **The Earth is covered with a crust of rock.** In some places, sections of crust have squeezed together, forcing their way upwards to make mountains. Mountains often form in a long line or group, called a mountain range. High up, it is cold and windy. This means that the tops of mountains are very icy, snowy and stormy.

Mount Everest 8849 metres (Asia)

Mount Kilimanjaro 5895 metres (Africa)

Aoraki/Mount Cook 3724 metres (Oceania)

27 **Mount Everest is the world's highest mountain.** It's on the border between Nepal and China, in the Himalayas mountain range. It is 8849 metres high. The first people to climb to the top of Everest were Edmund Hillary and Tenzing Norgay, on 29 May, 1953.

▼ Mount Everest is so high that climbers have to climb it over several days, stopping at camps along the way.

28 **The highest mountain on Earth isn't the hardest to climb.** Another peak, K2, is much tougher for mountaineers. At 8611 metres, it's the world's second-highest mountain. Its steep slopes and swirling storms make it incredibly dangerous. Fewer than 400 people have ever climbed it, and over 85 have died in the attempt.

▲ Edmund Hillary (left) and Tenzing Norgay, photographed in 1953, the year they became the first people to reach the summit of Mount Everest.

EARTH AND SPACE

Mount Aconcagua 6959 metres (South America)

Denali 6190 metres (North America)

Mount Blanc 4807 metres (Europe)

◀ This diagram shows a height comparison of the highest mountains by continent.

I DON'T BELIEVE IT!

Mountains seem big to us, but they're very small compared to the whole planet. If the world was shrunk to the size of a football, it would feel totally smooth.

29 Most mountains are shaped like big humps — but a cliff is a sheer drop. The east face of Great Trango, a mountain in Pakistan, is 1340 metres high, making it the tallest vertical cliff in the world. There's another giant cliff on Mount Thor in Canada, with a drop of 1250 metres. If a pebble fell off one of these cliffs, it would take more than 15 seconds to reach the bottom!

30 Some people don't just climb to the tops of high mountains — they live there! The town of Wenzhuan in Tibet, China, is the highest in the world. It is in the Himalayas, 5100 metres up — that's over 5 kilometres above sea level! The highest capital city is La Paz, in the Andes in Bolivia, South America.

▼ The city of La Paz in Bolivia is situated in the Andes mountains. It has an altitude (height) of around 3600 metres.

Hot volcanoes

31 Volcanoes happen because the Earth is hot inside. The surface is cool but under the crust, scorching semi-liquid rock called magma is under so much pressure that it is almost solid. The shifting of the crust sometimes releases pressure. This causes the magma to melt and push through cracks in the crust as a volcanic eruption.

▼ Here, an oceanic plate dips below a continental plate. The thinner oceanic plate is pushed down into the mantle.

Plates move together

Subducted plate melts into mantle

A volcano has formed along the edge of the overlying plate

I DON'T BELIEVE IT!
Tectonic plates move at about the same speed as your fingernails grow. That is just a few centimetres each year.

▼ Constructive boundaries often occur in the middle of oceans, forming ocean ridges.

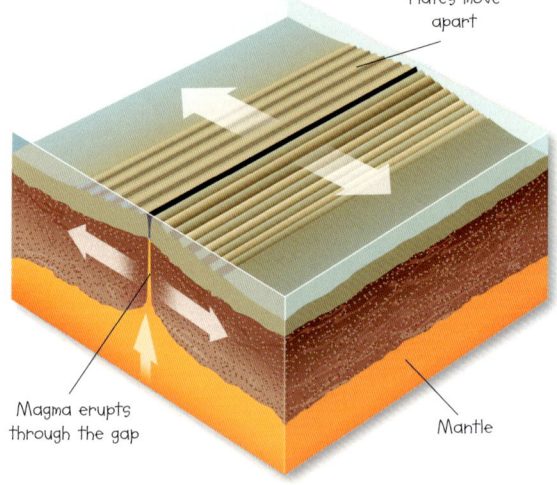

Plates move apart

Magma erupts through the gap

Mantle

32 The Earth's crust is cracked into giant pieces called tectonic plates. There are about 60 plates, and the seven largest are thousands of kilometres across. Tectonic plates move slowly across the Earth's surface. This movement, called continental drift, has caused the continents to move apart over millions of years.

EARTH AND SPACE

33 About 250 million years ago there was just one continent, known as Pangaea. The movement of tectonic plates broke Pangaea apart and moved the land around to form the continents we recognize today.

34 Most volcanoes erupt along plate boundaries. These are the cracks separating tectonic plates. On a world map of plate boundaries (below) you can see there are often rows of volcanoes along boundaries.

35 Volcanoes also happen at 'hot spots'. These are places where especially hot magma being driven upwards in the mantle, burns through the middle of a plate to form volcanoes. The most famous hot-spot volcanoes are those of the Hawaiian islands.

▼ Most active volcanoes occur along the 'Ring of Fire' (tinted red). Five volcanoes from around the world are highlighted on the map below.

Rivers and waterfalls

36 **The Earth is laced with thousands of rivers.** Rivers are channels of water that flow towards the sea. They allow the rain that falls on the land to drain away. Rivers also provide people and animals with drinking water and a place to wash, swim and find food. A waterfall is a place where a river flows over a rocky ledge and pours down to a lower level.

37 **The world's longest river is the Nile, in Africa.** It starts in the area near Lake Victoria and flows north to Egypt, where it opens into the Mediterranean Sea. The journey covers nearly 6700 kilometres, and about 3470 cubic metres of water flows out of the Nile every second. The Nile provides water, a transport route, and fishing for millions of people. If it wasn't for the Nile, the civilization of ancient Egypt could not have existed.

38 **Although the Nile is the longest river, the Amazon is the biggest.** The Amazon flows from west to east across South America, and empties into the Atlantic Ocean. It carries 58 times as much water as the Nile, and about 200,000 cubic metres flow out of it each second. In some places, the Amazon is 60 kilometres wide.

◀ This aerial photo of the River Amazon shows how it twists and loops as it flows through the Amazon rainforest in South America.

EARTH AND SPACE

▲ Part of the Grand Canyon, with the Colorado River visible at the bottom of a deep gorge.

▼ A waterfall forms where a river flows from hard rock onto softer rock. The softer rock is worn away faster, while the overhanging ledge of hard rock gradually crumbles away. Over time, the waterfall retreats, or moves upstream.

39 Angel Falls in Venezuela is the world's highest waterfall, spilling over a drop 979 metres high. It flows off the side of a very high, flat-topped mountain. Although it's the world's highest waterfall, it's not the biggest. Many waterfalls are much wider and carry more water – including Niagara Falls in North America and Victoria Falls in Africa.

40 Rivers can cut through solid rock. Over thousands of years, as a river flows, it wears away the rock around it. If the stone is quite soft, the river can carve a deep, steep-sided valley, or gorge. The Grand Canyon in Arizona, USA, is a massive gorge cut by the Colorado River. It is about 450 kilometres long, and in areas it is up to 29 kilometres wide and 1.8 kilometres deep.

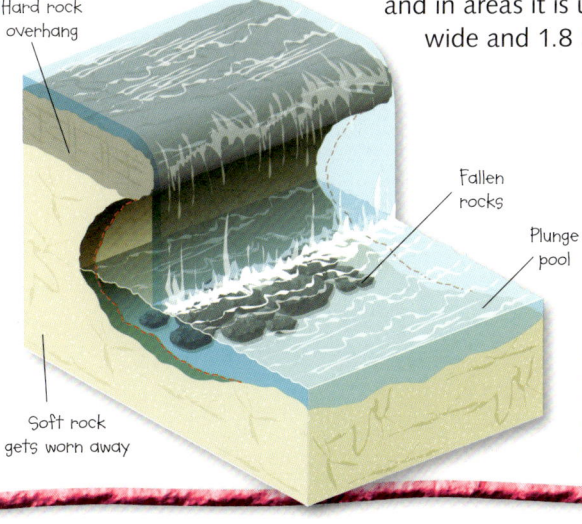

Hard rock overhang

Fallen rocks

Plunge pool

Soft rock gets worn away

▶ At Angel Falls, the world's highest waterfall, the water spreads out into a misty spray as it plunges down the cliff.

Dry deserts

41 **Deserts occur in places where it's hard for rain to reach.** Most rain comes from clouds that form over the sea and blow onto the land. If there's a big mountain range, the clouds never reach the other side and so an area called a rain shadow desert forms. Deserts also form in the middle of continents. The land there is so far from the sea, rain clouds rarely reach it.

▲ The Namib Desert in the southwest of Africa contains some of the biggest sand dunes in the world.

QUIZ

1. Which desert contains some of the world's biggest sand dunes?
2. How big is the Sahara?
3. Does an oasis contain saltwater?

Answers:
1. The Namib Desert in southwest Africa 2. Over 9 million square kilometres 3. No, it's a freshwater spring

42 **The world's biggest hot desert used to be a swamp!** The Sahara takes up most of northern Africa. It is made up of over 9 million square kilometres of dry sand, pebbles and boulders. There are some oases too, where freshwater springs flow out of the ground. Animal bones and objects left by ancient peoples show that around 6000 years ago, the Sahara was green and swampy. Lots of hippos, crocodiles and humans lived there.

Great Victoria Desert 424,000 km²
Kalahari Desert 930,000 km²
Gobi Desert 1,300,000 km²
Arabian Desert 2,330,000 km²
Sahara 9,269,000 km²

◀ These sand piles show the relative sizes of the world's biggest deserts.

EARTH AND SPACE

▲ Desert roses aren't plants. They occur when desert minerals, such as gypsum, combine with sand to form crystals.

43 **Deserts aren't always hot.** The hottest temperature ever recorded was 56.7°C in Death Valley, USA. However, deserts can be cold, too. The world's biggest desert is actually the continent of Antarctica. It is classed as a desert because it gets very little rain or snow. The coldest temperature ever recorded was -89.2°C, at an Antarctic station. All deserts can be cold at night, as there are no clouds to stop heat escaping.

▶ Sand dunes form in different shapes and patterns, depending on the type of wind and sand in the desert. The blue arrows indicate the wind direction.

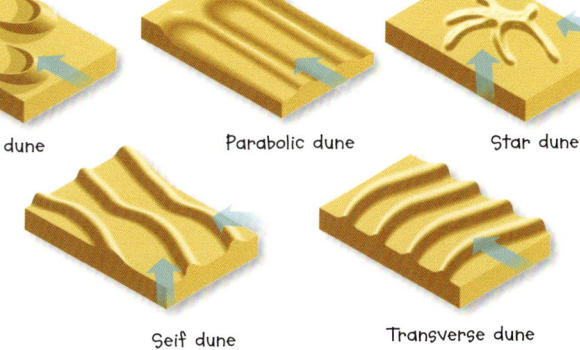

Barchan dune   Parabolic dune   Star dune

Seif dune   Transverse dune

44 **The Atacama desert in Chile, South America, is the driest in the world.** It lies between the Pacific Ocean and the Andes mountains. In South America, the winds blow from east to west. As the winds rise to cross the Andes, the air cools. Water vapour in the air condenses and turns to rain, falling before it reaches the desert on the other side. The Atacama is so dry that people who died there 9000 years ago have been preserved as mummies.

45 **Even in dry deserts, there is water if you know where to look.** Desert plants such as cactuses store water in their stems, leaves or spines. When rain does fall, it seeps into the ground and stays there. Desert people and animals chew desert plants or dig into the ground to find enough water.

▶ An oasis is a freshwater spring in a desert. Oases form when water stored deep underground meets a barrier of rock that it can't soak through, and rises to the desert surface.

fantastic forests

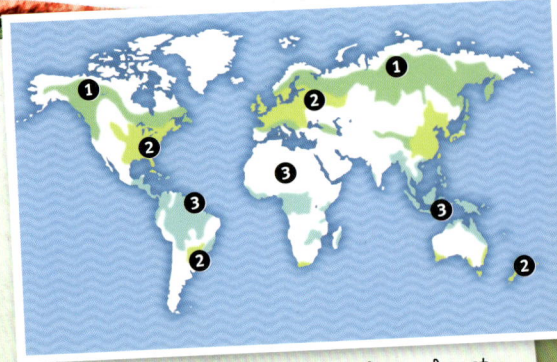

▲ This map shows the major areas of forest in the world:
① Coniferous forest
② Temperate forest
③ Tropical forest

46 There are three main kinds of forest. They are coniferous, temperate and tropical forests. Each grow in different regions of the world, depending on the climate.

47 Coniferous trees form huge forests around the northern part of the planet. They have long, green, needle-like leaves covered in a waxy coating. These trees stay in leaf throughout the year. In winter, the waxy surface helps snow slide off the leaves so that sunlight can reach them to keep them alive. Coniferous trees produce seeds in cones.

◀ Squirrels can open seed cones from coniferous trees in just a few seconds.

EARTH AND SPACE

48 Most trees in temperate forests have flat, broad leaves and need large amounts of water to keep them alive. In winter, the trees cannot get enough water from the frozen ground, so they lose their leaves and grow new ones in spring. Deer, rabbits, foxes and mice live on the woodland floor while squirrels, woodpeckers and owls live in the trees.

▲ A jaguar stalks through a dense tropical forest in Belize.

49 Large numbers of trees grow close together in a tropical forest. They have broad, evergreen leaves and branches that almost touch. These form a leafy roof over the forest called a canopy. It rains almost every day in a tropical rainforest. The vegetation is so thick, it can take a raindrop ten minutes to reach the ground. Three-quarters of all known animal and plant species live in rainforests. They include huge spiders, brightly coloured frogs and jungle cats.

▲ The Hoh temperate rainforest in Washington state, USA, is home to elks, bears and cougars.

QUIZ

1. What are the three main kinds of forest?
2. Which types of tree produce seeds in cones?
3. In which kind of forest would you find brightly coloured frogs?

Answers:
1. Coniferous, temperate and tropical 2. Coniferous trees 3. Tropical rainforest

25

What is a rainforest?

50 Rainforests are places where lots of rain falls every year – usually more than 2000 millimetres. They are filled with enormous, broad-leaved trees and a bewildering collection of living things. Rainforests usually grow in warm, steamy parts of the world.

51 Trees provide habitats (homes) for millions of rainforest animals and plants. Much of the wildlife in these forests cannot survive anywhere else – just one of the reasons why rainforests need to be protected.

Toco toucan

52 Of all the different habitats found on Earth, rainforests have the biggest range of living things. They are home to more than 80 percent of all insects and a single rainforest in South America has 18,000 different types of plants. The word 'biodiversity' is used to describe the range of living things that live in one habitat.

Tapir

EARTH AND SPACE

Queen Alexandra's birdwing butterfly

53 **Rainforests have four main layers.** The bottom layers are the dark, dank forest floor and understorey, where the shortest plants live. Here, bugs, frogs, fungi and many other living things thrive. The middle layer is the forest canopy and the top layer is the emergent layer. This is where the tallest trees poke up above a blanket of green leaves. The trees are home to vines, mosses, monkeys, lizards, snakes, insects and thousands of species (types) of bird.

◀ Most animals and plants live in the rainforest canopy layer. The understorey is very gloomy because not much sunlight reaches it.

I DON'T BELIEVE IT!
People who live in rainforests can build their entire homes from plant materials. Walls are made from palm stems or bamboo and leaves can be woven to make roofs and floors.

Red-eyed tree frog

54 **Rainforests are home to people as well as animals and plants.** Many tribes (groups of people) live in these dense, green forests around the world, finding food, medicines and shelter amongst the trees. Some of them still follow a traditional lifestyle, hunting animals and gathering plants for food.

The ends of the Earth

55 **The Earth is round, but it has two 'ends' — the North Pole and the South Pole.** The Earth is constantly spinning around an imaginary line called the axis. At the ends of this axis are the poles. Here, it is always cold, because the poles are so far from the Sun.

▲ The position of the poles means they receive little heat from the Sun.

56 **At the North Pole, the average temperature is −20°C.** At the South pole, it's much colder — about -50°C. It's hard for humans to survive in this cold. Water droplets in your breath would freeze on your face. If you were to touch something made of metal with your bare hand, it would freeze onto your skin and stick there.

57 **The area around the North Pole is called the Arctic.** It consists of the Arctic Ocean and parts of Europe, Asia and North America that surround it. Many animals live in the Arctic. Polar bears and seals live on the sea ice and Arctic foxes, Arctic hares and snowy owls live on the land. The Arctic Ocean is mostly covered by ice, but the amount of ice is decreasing each year due to global warming. Pollution in the air is trapping heat close to the Earth, making it warm up.

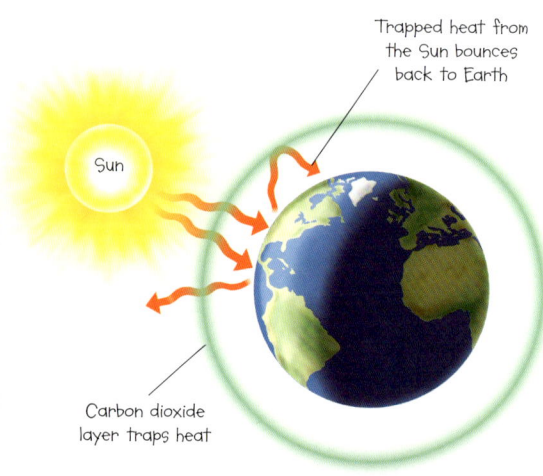

◀ Pollution in the form of carbon dioxide and other gases traps heat from the Sun, making the Earth warm up. This is one reason that the polar ice is melting.

▲ There are several different species (types) of penguins living in Antarctica. These emperor penguins and their chicks are the largest species.

58 **The Antarctic is mostly made up of a huge continent, called Antarctica.** Much of it is covered in a layer of solid ice up to 4.7 kilometres thick. The Antarctic is colder than the Arctic because its thick ice and mountains make it very high, and the air is colder higher up. Because Antarctica is so big, the seas around it cannot warm it very much. Antarctica is home to wildlife such as penguins, seals, seabirds and fish.

I DON'T BELIEVE IT!

Explorers at the poles sometimes lose body parts. If they let their fingers, toes or nose get too cold, they can get frostbite. Blood stops flowing to these parts, and they can turn black and fall off.

59 **Explorers didn't make it to the poles until the 20th century.** US explorer Robert Peary and his team reached the North Pole in 1909. Soon afterwards, two explorers raced to reach the South Pole. Norwegian Roald Amundsen arrived first, in December 1911. British explorer Robert Scott arrived one month later – but he and his men died on their way home.

◀ There are no towns or cities in Antarctica as it's so cold, but people do go there to explore and to study nature. They sometimes use snowmobiles to travel around on the snow and ice.

Amazing oceans

Continental slope · Land · Continental shelf · Spreading ridge · Abyssal trench · Abyssal hills

60 **About 70 percent of the Earth's surface is covered by ocean.** The oceans cover about 361 million square kilometres and they are all connected. The average depth of the ocean is 3750 metres. Over 90 percent of the Earth's species (types) of living things live in the oceans.

61 **The deepest point in all the world's oceans is called Challenger Deep.** It is in the Mariana Trench in the Pacific Ocean and is 10,923 metres deep – almost 11 kilometres. A tower of 3500 elephants, one on top of the next, could stand in it without touching the surface. In 1960, two explorers, Jacques Piccard and Don Walsh, visited the bottom of Challenger Deep in a diving vessel called *Trieste*.

62 **If you were sitting at the bottom of the deep ocean, you'd be squashed flat.** At great depths, the weight of all the water above presses from all sides. At the bottom of Challenger Deep, the water pressure is more than 1000 times stronger than at the surface. It's cold, too – only just above freezing point. People can only go there inside specially built diving machines with thick walls that can resist the pressure and cold.

◀ *Trieste* spent 20 minutes at the bottom of the Mariana Trench.

INDIAN OCEAN

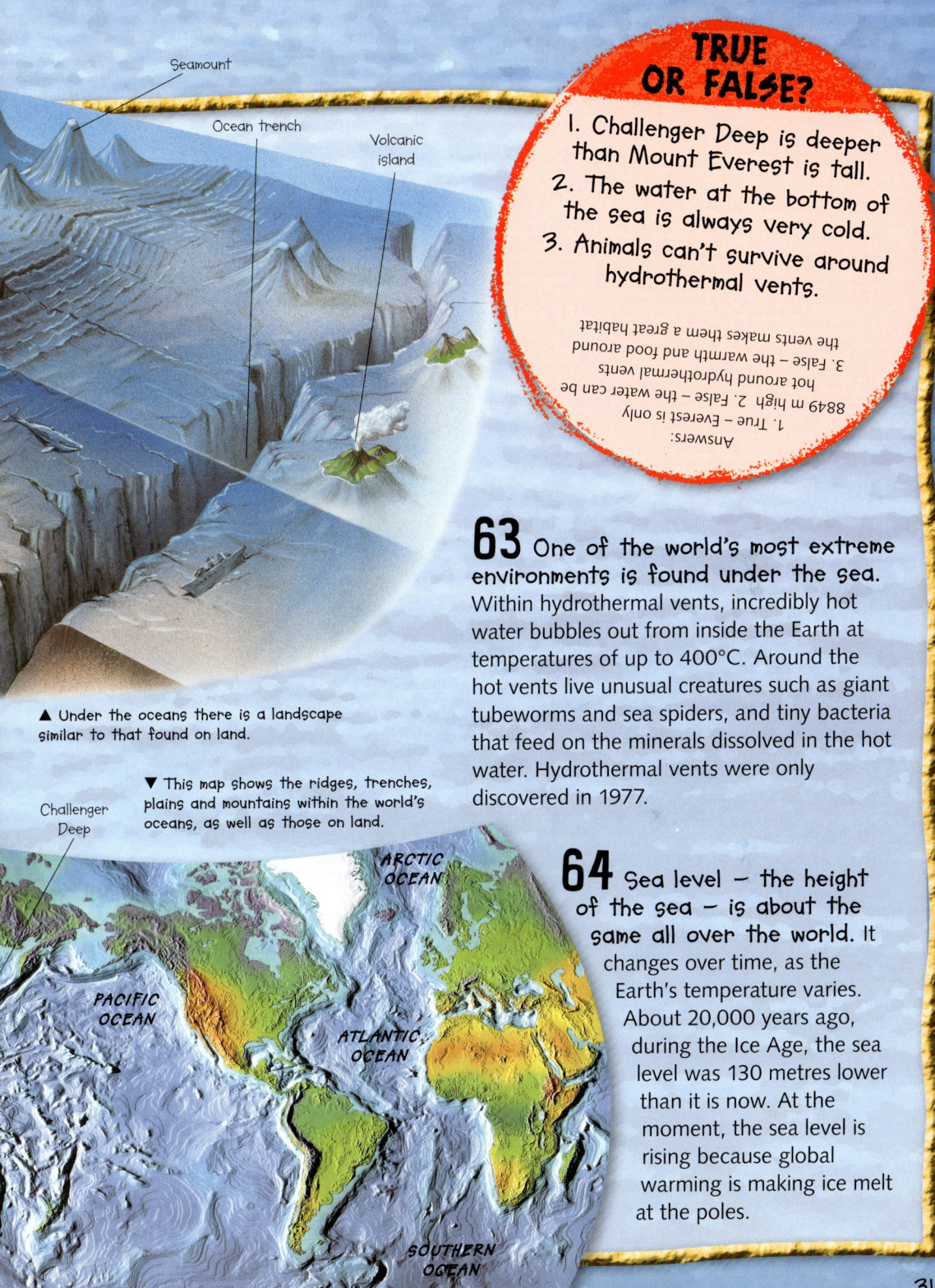

Seamount

Ocean trench

Volcanic island

▲ Under the oceans there is a landscape similar to that found on land.

Challenger Deep

▼ This map shows the ridges, trenches, plains and mountains within the world's oceans, as well as those on land.

ARCTIC OCEAN

PACIFIC OCEAN

ATLANTIC OCEAN

SOUTHERN OCEAN

TRUE OR FALSE?

1. Challenger Deep is deeper than Mount Everest is tall.
2. The water at the bottom of the sea is always very cold.
3. Animals can't survive around hydrothermal vents.

Answers:
1. True – Everest is only 8849 m high 2. False – the water can be hot around hydrothermal vents 3. False – the warmth and food around the vents makes them a great habitat

63 One of the world's most extreme environments is found under the sea. Within hydrothermal vents, incredibly hot water bubbles out from inside the Earth at temperatures of up to 400°C. Around the hot vents live unusual creatures such as giant tubeworms and sea spiders, and tiny bacteria that feed on the minerals dissolved in the hot water. Hydrothermal vents were only discovered in 1977.

64 Sea level – the height of the sea – is about the same all over the world. It changes over time, as the Earth's temperature varies. About 20,000 years ago, during the Ice Age, the sea level was 130 metres lower than it is now. At the moment, the sea level is rising because global warming is making ice melt at the poles.

Our atmosphere

65 Earth is wrapped in a blanket of air called the atmosphere, which is hundreds of kilometres thick. The atmosphere keeps heat in at night, and during the day forms a sunscreen, protecting us from the Sun's fierce rays. Without it there would be no weather.

66 Most weather happens in the troposphere. This is the layer of atmosphere that stretches from the ground to around 10 kilometres above your head. The higher in the troposphere you go, the cooler the air. Because of this, clouds are most likely to form here. Clouds with flattened tops show just where the troposphere meets the next layer, the stratosphere.

KEY
1. Exosphere 190 to 960 kilometres
2. Thermosphere 80 to 190 kilometres
3. Mesosphere 50 to 80 kilometres
4. Stratosphere 10 to 50 kilometres
5. Troposphere 0 to 10 kilometres

Low-level satellites orbit within the exosphere

The Northern and Southern Lights – the auroras – are formed in the thermosphere

Meteors entering the atmosphere burn up in the mesosphere, causing 'shooting stars'

Aeroplanes either fly high in the troposphere, or in the lower levels of the stratosphere

Weather forms in the troposphere

▶ This view of the Earth from the International Space Station, which orbits the Earth, shows the atmosphere as a thin, wispy layer.

▲ The atmosphere stretches right into space. Scientists have split it into five layers, or spheres.

EARTH AND SPACE

67 Molecules (tiny particles) in the air are constantly bumping into each other. The more they do this, the greater the air pressure. There are usually more collisions lower in the troposphere, because gravity pulls the molecules towards Earth's surface. The higher you go, the lower the air pressure, and the less oxygen there is in the air.

▼ At high altitudes there is less oxygen. That is why mountaineers have to give their bodies time to adjust as they climb.

68 **Warmth makes air move.** When heat from the Sun warms the molecules in air, they move faster and spread out more. This makes the air lighter, so it rises in the sky, creating low pressure. As it gets higher, the air cools. The molecules slow down and become heavier again, so they start to sink back to Earth.

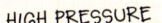

HIGH PRESSURE

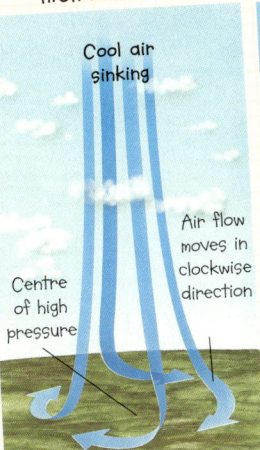

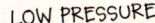

LOW PRESSURE

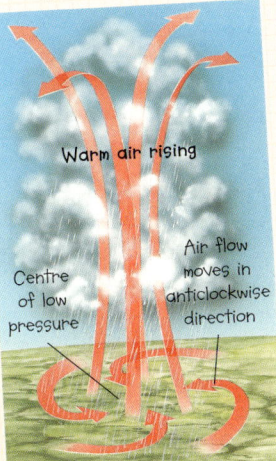

▲ A high pressure weather system gives us warmer weather, while low pressure gives us cooler, more unsettled weather. (In the Northern Hemisphere, air flows anticlockwise in a low pressure system, and clockwise in high pressure. In the Southern Hemisphere, it is the opposite.)

Clouds and rain

69 Water goes on a journey called the water cycle. As the Sun heats the ocean's surface, some seawater turns to vapour and rises. As it rises, it cools and turns back into droplets, which join to make clouds. The droplets continue forming bigger drops and eventually fall as rain. Some is soaked up by land, but a lot finds its way back to the sea.

KEY
1. Water evaporates from the sea
2. Clouds form
3. Water is given off by trees
4. Rain falls, filling rivers
5. Rivers run back to the sea

70 Some mountains are so tall that their summits are hidden by cloud. They can even affect the weather. When moving air hits a mountain slope it is forced upwards, causing its temperature to drop, and clouds to form.

▼ The peak of Chapaeva, in the Tian Shan mountain range in Asia, can be seen above the clouds.

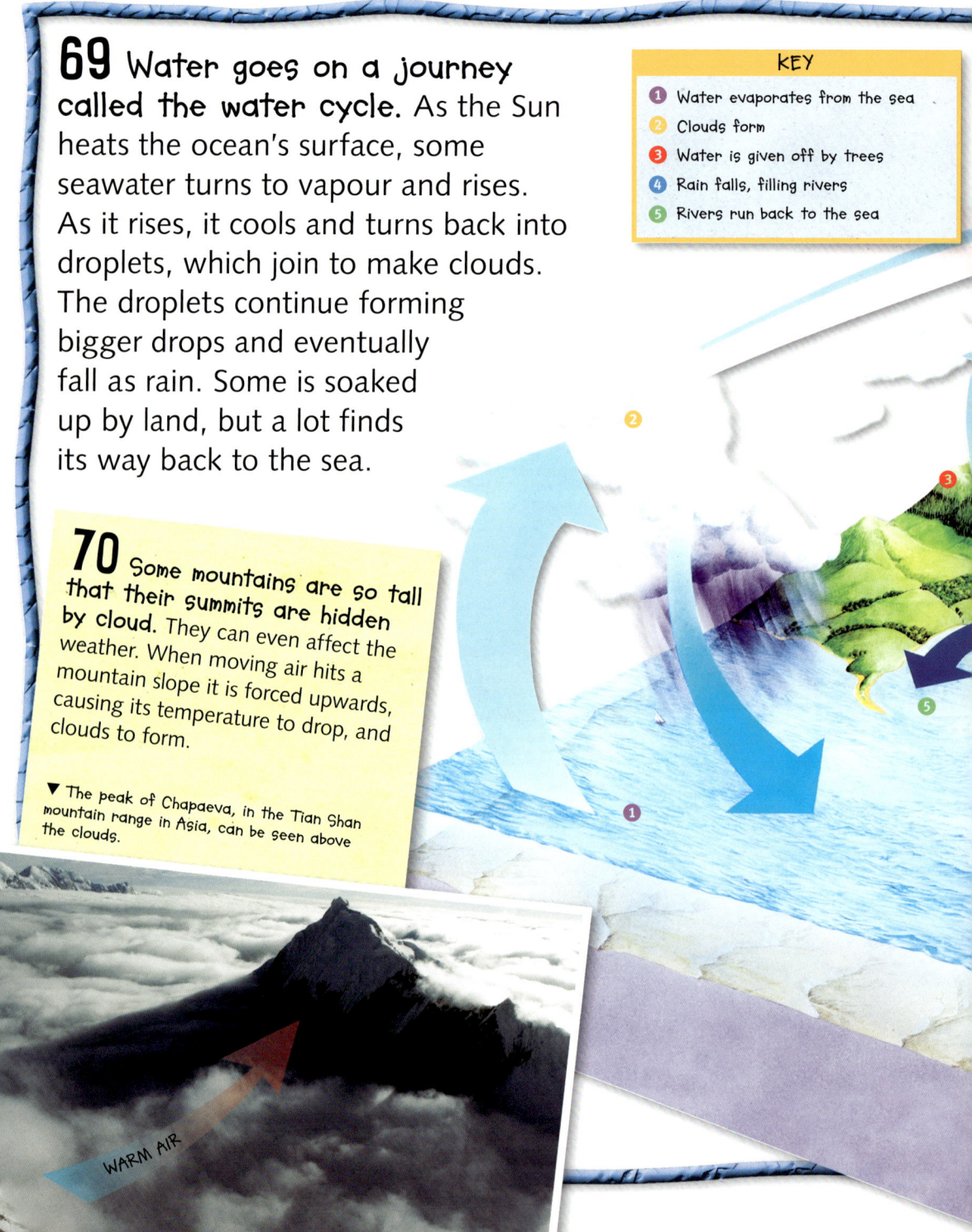

WARM AIR

EARTH AND SPACE

▼ Water moves in a continuous cycle between the ocean, atmosphere and land.

71 Clouds release energy. When water vapour becomes water droplets and forms clouds, a small amount of heat energy is given out into the atmosphere. Then, when the droplets fall as rain, kinetic (movement) energy is released as the rain hits the ground.

72 Clouds come in all shapes and sizes. Scientists divide them into three basic types according to their shape and height above the ground. Wispy cirrus clouds form high in the troposphere and rarely mean rain. Flat, layered stratus clouds may produce drizzle or a sprinkling of snow. Soft, fluffy cumulus clouds usually bring rain.

▶ Virga happens when rain reaches a layer of dry air. The rain droplets turn back into water vapour in mid-air, and seem to disappear.

73 Some rain never reaches the ground. The raindrops turn back into water vapour because they hit a layer of super-dry air. You can actually see the drops falling like a curtain from the cloud, but the curtain stops in mid-air. This type of weather is called virga.

Thunderbolts and lightning

74 **Thunderstorms are most likely to occur in summer.** Warm, moist air rises and forms cumulonimbus clouds. Inside the clouds, water droplets and ice crystals move about, building up positive and negative electrical charges. Electricity flows between the charges, creating a flash (lightning). The air heated by the lightning expands, causing a loud noise, or thunderclap.

▼ Cloud-to-cloud lightning is called sheet lightning. Lightning travelling from the cloud to the ground, as shown here, is called fork lightning.

I DON'T BELIEVE IT!
At any one time, there are around 2000 thunderstorms happening on Earth. Lightning strikes somewhere in the world about 100 times every second.

▼ Dramatic lightning flashes in Arizona, USA, light up the sky.

75 **Lightning comes in different colours.** If there is rain in the thundercloud, the lightning looks red or pink, and if there's hail, it looks blue. Lightning can also be yellow or white.

▼ Hailstones can be huge! These ones are as big as a golf ball.

76 Chunks of ice called hailstones can fall from thunderclouds. The biggest hailstones fell in Gopaljang, Bangladesh, in 1986 and weighed one kilogram each!

77 A person can survive a lightning strike. Lightning is very dangerous and can give a big enough electric shock to kill you. However, an American park ranger called Roy Sullivan survived being struck seven times.

78 Tall buildings are protected from lightning. Church steeples and other tall structures are often struck by bolts of lightning. This could damage the building, or give electric shocks to people inside, so lightning conductors are placed on the roof. These channel the lightning safely away.

◄ If lightning hits a conductor it is carried safely to the ground.

Howling hurricanes

▲ Hurricanes can cause widespread devastation and extreme flooding.

79 A hurricane is a huge, swirling mass of stormclouds. Hurricanes form over the ocean, but often travel onto land where they cause floods and destroy whole towns. A typical hurricane is about 500 kilometres wide. In the middle is a small, circular area with no clouds in it, about 70 kilometres wide. This is called the 'eye' of the hurricane.

80 Hurricanes begin in the tropics where the ocean is warm. The ocean surface has to be about 27°C or warmer for a hurricane to start. Warm, wet air rises, forming rainclouds. These begin to swirl in a spiral, caused by the spinning Earth. If the winds reach 118 kilometres an hour, the storm is called a hurricane. Hurricane winds can be as fast as 240 kilometres an hour.

81 The scientific name for this type of storm is a tropical cyclone. The word hurricane is only used for storms in the Atlantic and eastern North Pacific Oceans. The same type of storm in the western North Pacific is called a typhoon. In the Indian and South Pacific Oceans it is called a cyclone.

I DON'T BELIEVE IT!
Surrounding the eye of the hurricane is the eyewall. This is a mass of severe thunderstorms where most of the worst weather occurs.

EARTH AND SPACE

82 Most hurricanes rage harmlessly over the ocean. If they hit land, less powerful, slow-moving hurricanes can cause more damage than stronger hurricanes, which die out more quickly.

83 Hurricanes and other tropical cyclones can cause terrible disasters. When Hurricane Katrina struck the southern coast of the USA in August 2005, it damaged many cities on the coasts of Mississippi and Louisiana. In New Orleans, huge waves broke through the flood barriers and more than 80 percent of the city was flooded. The hurricane killed over 1800 people and caused damage costing over $80 billion. The Bhola cyclone, which hit Bangladesh in 1970, killed over 300,000 people.

▲ A satellite view from space showing a hurricane swirling across the Gulf of Mexico.

84 Scientists think hurricanes are getting worse. Global warming means that the Earth's temperature is rising, so the seas are getting warmer. This means that more hurricanes are likely. Hurricanes are also becoming bigger and more powerful, as there is more heat energy to fuel them.

▼ These buildings near Lake Pontchartrain, Louisiana, USA, were destroyed by Hurricane Katrina in 2005.

Twisting tornadoes

85 **Tornadoes are also called twisters.** A tornado is an incredibly powerful windstorm that twists around in a swirling 'vortex' shape. It forms a narrow funnel or tube, stretching from the clouds to the ground. Tornadoes often look dark because of all the dirt, dust and broken objects that they pick up as they travel across the land.

86 **You can sometimes tell when a tornado is coming, because the sky turns green.** Tornadoes usually develop from thunderclouds. Scientists are not sure exactly how they form. They think that as warm, damp air rises, drier, colder air is pulled in and begins to swirl around it. This creates a spinning tube of wind that moves along the ground. A tornado can travel at up to 80 kilometres an hour.

87 **Tornadoes contain some of the fastest winds on the planet.** Wind inside a tornado can move at up to 500 kilometres an hour. This powerful wind can cause terrible damage. Tornadoes smash buildings, tear off roofs, make bridges collapse, and suck out doors and windows. They can pick up people, animals and cars, and carry them through the air.

Cold front

Warm front

◄ Tornadoes often form where a front, or mass, of cold air meets warm air. They spin around each other and form a funnel shape.

EARTH AND SPACE

I DON'T BELIEVE IT!
During a 'super outbreak' in the USA in April 2011, 207 tornadoes happened in a single day.

◀ A large, terrifying tornado snakes down to the ground from the base of a big thundercloud.

88 Damaging tornadoes happen most often in **Tornado Alley**. This is an area which stretches across the middle of the USA, between the states of Texas and Illinois. Tornadoes are most common there in the tornado season, from April to August. The Great Tri-State Tornado of 1925 was one of the worst ever. It roared through Missouri, Illionois and Indiana, travelling 350 kilometres. It destroyed 15,000 homes and killed 695 people.

◀ The shaded area on this map shows the part of the USA known as Tornado Alley, where tornadoes are most common.

89 Sometimes, tornadoes occur in deserts, or over the sea. In sandy deserts, small tornadoes pick up sand and carry it along in a whirling tower. They are called sand devils or dust devils. Tornadoes over the sea can suck up water in the same way, and carry it for long distances. They are known as waterspouts.

flooding the land

90 A flood happens when water overflows and covers what is normally land. Floods can be caused by rivers overflowing their banks after heavy rain. The sea can also flood the land with large waves or tsunamis. Floods can be useful – some rivers flood every year in the rainy season, bringing water and mud that make farmland moist and fertile. However, most floods are bad news.

▲ A satellite image of the River Nile in Egypt flowing into the Mediterranean Sea. The green triangular area is the Nile Delta. The Nile used to flood each summer, spreading fertile silt across the land. These floods are now controlled by the Aswan Dam in southern Egypt.

▼ A woman carries a precious pot of clean drinking water through dirty floodwaters during a flood in Bangladesh in 1998.

91 Floods can cause death and destruction. When floodwater flows into houses, it fills them with mud, rubbish and sewage (smelly waste from drains and toilets). It ruins electrical appliances, carpets and furniture. After a flood, homes have to be completely cleaned out and repaired – costing huge amounts of money. Even worse, fast-flowing floodwater can sweep away people, cars and even buildings.

EARTH AND SPACE

I DON'T BELIEVE IT!

The Bible tells of a great flood that covered the world in water. Some scientists think flood stories may be based on flooding that happened around 10,000 years ago, as sea levels rose when ice melted after the last Ice Age.

92 **Floods often cause water shortages.** Although there's water everywhere, it's dirty and not safe to drink. The dirty water can fill up water supply pipes and water treatment works. They can't supply clean water, and the taps have to be switched off. During bad floods, the emergency services have to deliver water in bottles or tanks, so that people have enough clean water to drink.

93 **More floods are coming.** Because of global warming, the Earth is heating up. In some areas, this means more water will evaporate into the air, causing more clouds and more rain. Global warming also means higher sea levels, so more areas of land are at risk of being flooded.

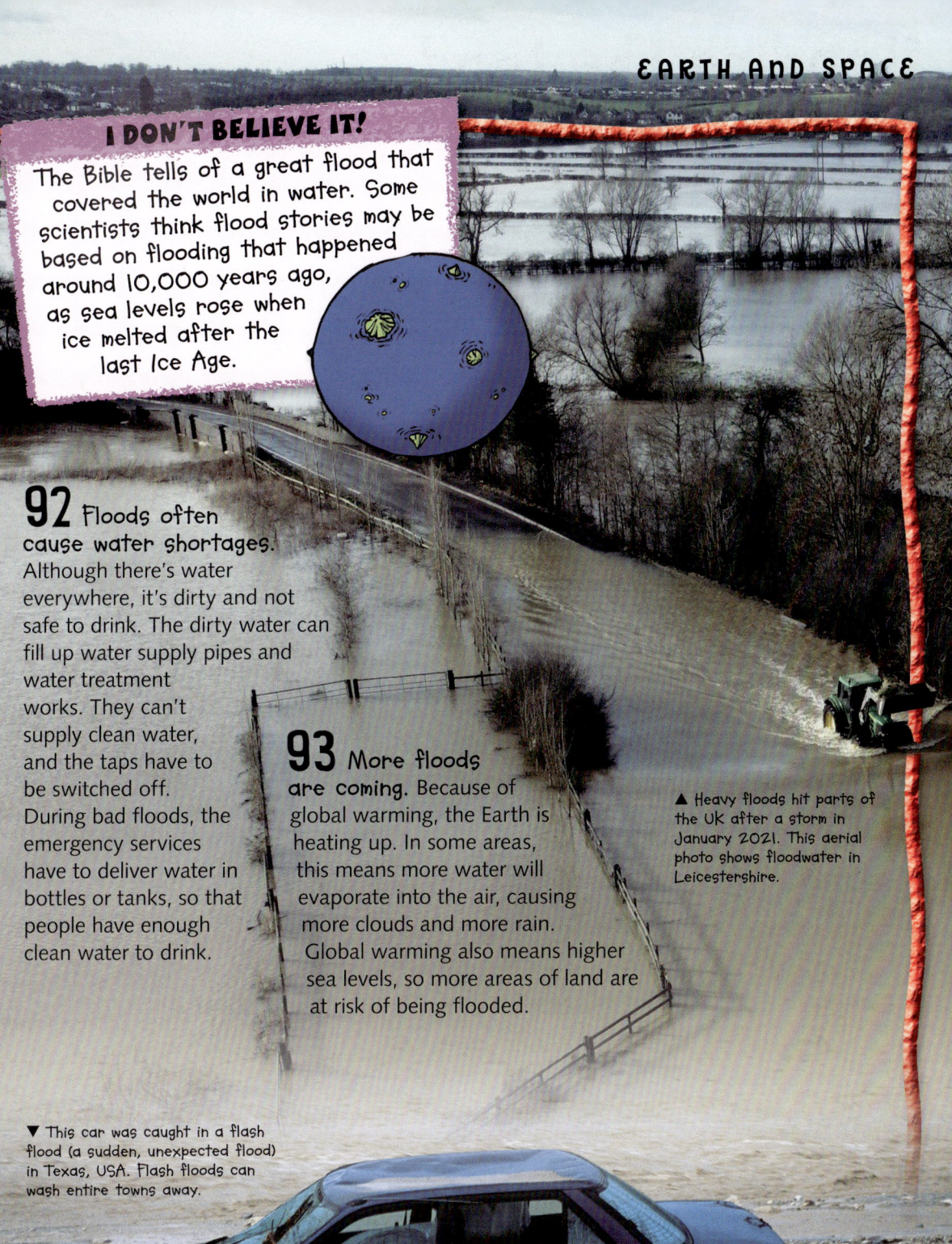

▲ Heavy floods hit parts of the UK after a storm in January 2021. This aerial photo shows floodwater in Leicestershire.

▼ This car was caught in a flash flood (a sudden, unexpected flood) in Texas, USA. Flash floods can wash entire towns away.

SCIENCE

94 **Even one hundred books like this could not explain all the reasons why we need science.** Toasters, bicycles, mobile phones, computers, cars, light bulbs – all the gadgets and machines we use every day are the results of scientific discoveries. Houses, skyscrapers, bridges and rockets are built using science. Our knowledge of medicines, illnesses and the human body comes from science.

▼ In a big city, science is all around you — everything from sky-scraping buildings to speedy vehicles and useful gadgets is based on science and technology.

Small science

95 **Everything is made up of atoms.** They are the smallest bits of a substance. They are so tiny, even a billion atoms would be too small to see. But scientists have carried out experiments to find out what's inside an atom. The answer is – even smaller bits. These are sub-atomic particles, and there are three main kinds.

97 **At the centre of each atom is a blob called the nucleus.** It contains two kinds of sub-atomic particles. These are protons and neutrons. Protons are positive, or plus. The neutron is neither positive nor negative. Around the centre of each atom are sub-atomic particles called electrons. They whizz round the nucleus. In the same way that a proton in the nucleus is positive or plus, an electron is negative or minus. The number of protons and electrons is usually the same.

96 **Atoms of the various elements have different numbers of protons and neutrons.** An atom of hydrogen has just one proton. An atom of helium, the gas put in party balloons to make them float, has two protons and two neutrons. An atom of the heavy metal called lead has 82 protons and 124 neutrons.

I DON'T BELIEVE IT!
One hundred years ago, people thought the electrons were spread out in an atom, like the raisins in a raisin pudding.

▶ The bits inside an atom give each substance its features, from exploding hydrogen to life-giving oxygen.

Hydrogen Helium Oxygen

• Electron
• Proton
• Neutron

SCIENCE

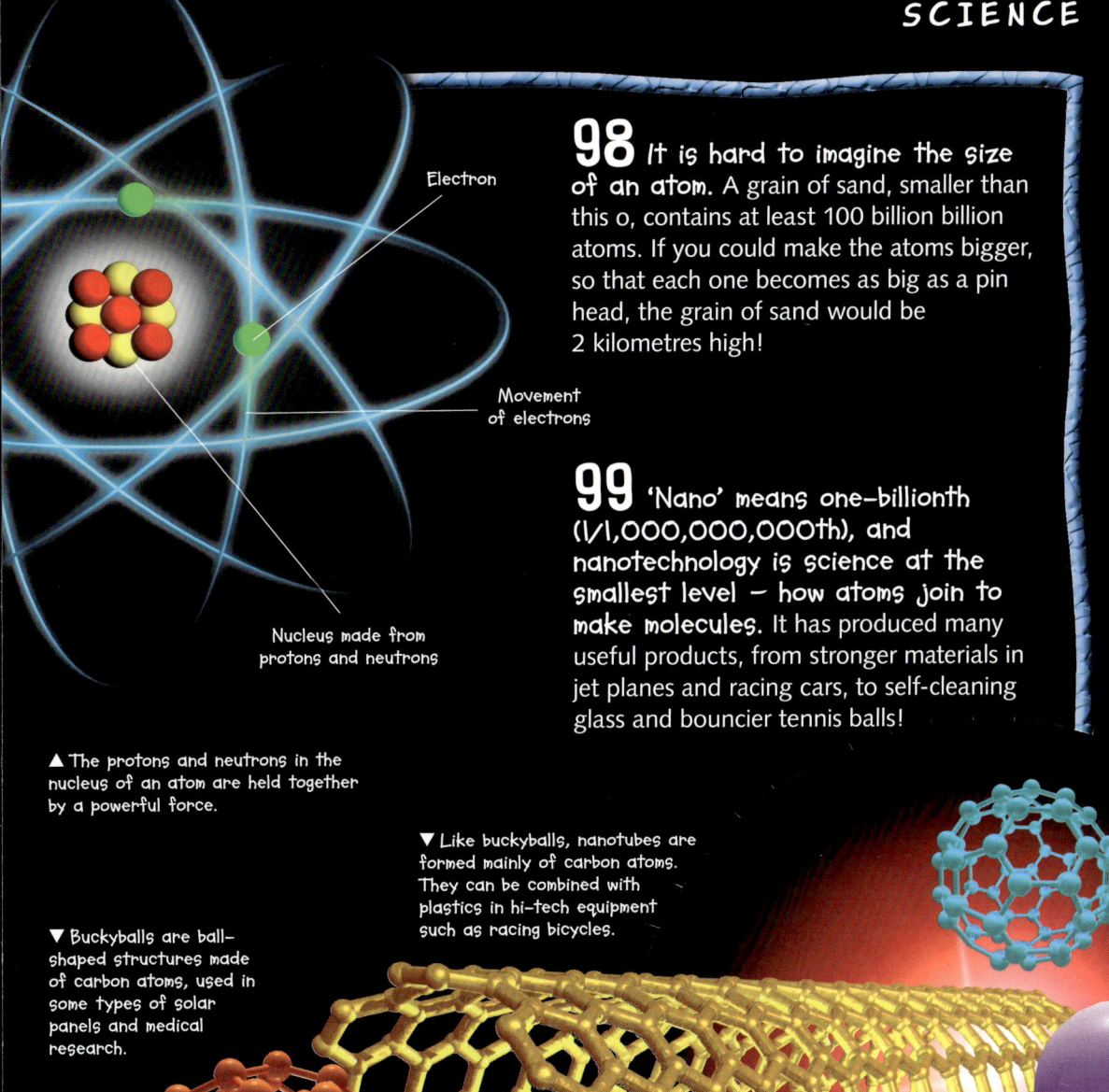

Electron

Movement of electrons

Nucleus made from protons and neutrons

98 **It is hard to imagine the size of an atom.** A grain of sand, smaller than this o, contains at least 100 billion billion atoms. If you could make the atoms bigger, so that each one becomes as big as a pin head, the grain of sand would be 2 kilometres high!

99 **'Nano' means one-billionth (1/1,000,000,000th), and nanotechnology is science at the smallest level – how atoms join to make molecules.** It has produced many useful products, from stronger materials in jet planes and racing cars, to self-cleaning glass and bouncier tennis balls!

▲ The protons and neutrons in the nucleus of an atom are held together by a powerful force.

▼ Buckyballs are ball-shaped structures made of carbon atoms, used in some types of solar panels and medical research.

▼ Like buckyballs, nanotubes are formed mainly of carbon atoms. They can be combined with plastics in hi-tech equipment such as racing bicycles.

When science is hot!

100 **Fire! Flames! Burning! Heat!** The science of heat is important in all kinds of ways. Not only do we cook with heat, but we also warm our homes and heat water. Burning happens in all kinds of engines in cars, trucks, planes and rockets. It is also used in factory processes, from making steel to shaping plastics.

▲ A firework burns suddenly as an explosive, producing heat, light and sound. The 'bang' is the sound made by the paper wrapper as it is blown apart.

Heat from the drink is conducted up the metal spoon

101 **Heat can move by conduction.** A hot object will pass on, or transfer, some of its heat to a cooler one. Dip a metal spoon in a hot drink and the spoon handle soon warms up. Heat is conducted from the drink, through the metal.

102 **Heat moves by invisible 'heat rays'.** This is called thermal radiation and the rays are infrared waves. Our planet is warmed by the Sun because heat from the Sun radiates through space as infrared waves.

TRUE OR FALSE?

1. Burning happens inside the engine of a plane.
2. A device for measuring temperature is called a calendar.
3. Heat rays are known as infrablue waves.

Answers:
1. True 2. False 3. False

◀ Heat is the energy of molecules (tiny particles) moving. Metal is a good conductor of heat. Materials such as plastic and wood are poor conductors.

SCIENCE

103 **Burning, also called combustion, is a chemical process.** Oxygen gas from the air joins to, or combines with, the substance being burned. The chemical change releases lots of heat, and usually light too. If this happens really fast, we call it an explosion.

▲ A burner flame makes glass so hot it becomes soft and bendy, so it can be stretched, shaped and even blown up like a balloon.

104 **Temperature is a measure of how hot or cold something is.** It is usually measured in degrees Celsius (°C) or Fahrenheit (°F). Water freezes at 0°C (32°F), and boils at 100°C (212°F). We use thermometers to take our temperatures. Your body temperature is about 37°C (98.6°F).

▶ This thermometer contains alcohol coloured by a red dye. As it warms, the alcohol expands (takes up more space). It moves up the thin tube, showing the temperature on the scale.

105 **Heat moves through liquids and gases by convection.** Some of the liquid or gas takes in heat, gets lighter, and rises into cooler areas. Then other cooler liquid or gas moves in to do the same and the process repeats. You can see this as 'wavy' hot air rising from a flame.

▶ Hot air shimmering over a candle is a visible sign of the heat being convected away.

49

Looking at light

106 **Almost everything you do depends on light and the science of light, which is called optics.** Light is a form of energy that you can see. Light waves are made of electricity and magnetism – and they are tiny. About 2000 of them laid end to end would stretch across this full stop.

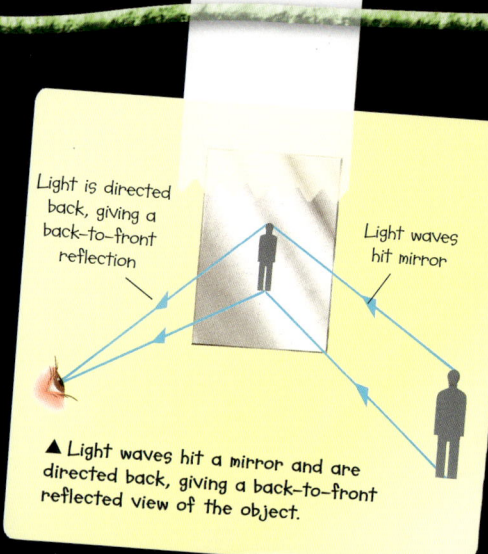

▲ Light waves hit a mirror and are directed back, giving a back-to-front reflected view of the object.

▲ A prism of clear glass or clear plastic separates the colours in white light.

107 **Like sound, light bounces off surfaces that are very smooth.** This is called reflection. A mirror is smooth, hard and flat. When you look at it, you see your reflection.

108 **Ordinary light from the Sun or from a light bulb is called white light.** But when white light passes through a prism, a triangular block of clear glass, it splits into many colours. These colours are known as the spectrum. Each colour has a different length of wave. A rainbow is made by raindrops, which work like millions of tiny prisms to split up sunlight.

SCIENCE

109 **Light passes through certain materials, like clear glass and plastic.** Materials that let light pass through, to give a clear view, are transparent. Those that do not allow light through, like wood and metal, are opaque.

110 **Mirrors and lenses are important parts of many optical (light-using) gadgets.** They are found in cameras, binoculars, microscopes, telescopes and lasers. Without them, we would have no close-up photographs of tiny microchips or insects or giant planets – in fact, no photos at all.

I DON'T BELIEVE IT!

Light is the fastest thing in the Universe – it travels through space at 300,000 kilometres per second. That's seven times around the world in less than one second!

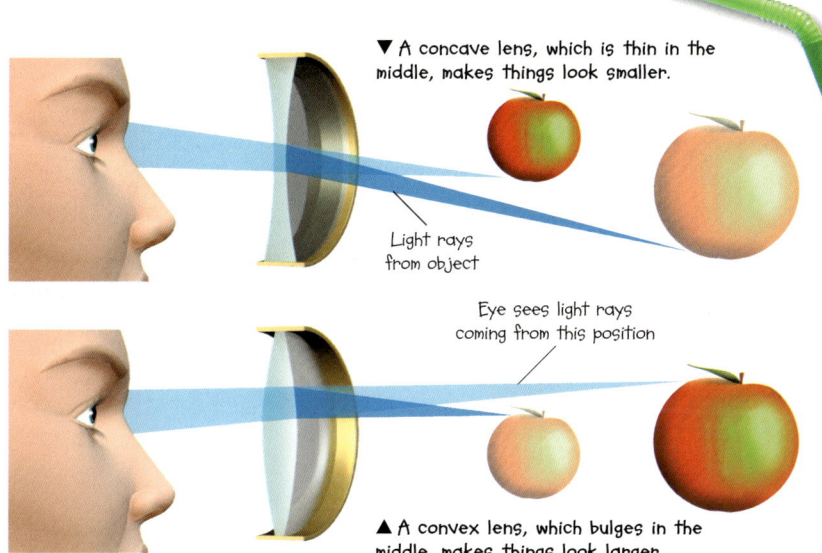

▼ A concave lens, which is thin in the middle, makes things look smaller.

Light rays from object

Eye sees light rays coming from this position

▲ A convex lens, which bulges in the middle, makes things look larger.

▲ Glass and water bend, or refract, light waves. This makes a drinking straw look bent where it goes behind the glass and then into the water.

111 **Light does not usually go straight through glass.** It bends slightly where it goes into the glass, then bends back as it comes out. This is called refraction. A lens is a curved piece of glass or plastic that bends light to make things look bigger, smaller or clearer. Spectacle and contact lenses bend light to help people see more clearly.

Mysterious magnets

112 Without magnets there would be no electric motors, computers or loudspeakers. Magnetism is an invisible force to do with atoms – tiny particles that make up everything. Atoms are made of even smaller particles, including electrons. Magnetism is linked to the way that these line up and move. Most magnetic substances contain iron. As iron makes up a big part of the metallic substance steel, steel is also magnetic.

▶ For metal recycling, an electromagnet lifts out only iron-containing or ferrous metals, such as steel.

113 A magnet is a lump of iron or steel that has all its electrons and atoms lined up. This means that their magnetic forces all add up. The force surrounds the magnet, in a region called the magnetic field. This is strongest at the two parts of the magnet called the poles.

▲ Maglev (magnetic levitation) trains use pushing or repelling magnetic forces to 'float' above their track.

SCIENCE

114 **A magnet has two different poles – north and south.** A north pole repels (pushes away) the north pole of another magnet. Two south poles also repel each other. But a north pole and a south pole attract (pull together). Both magnetic poles attract any substance containing iron, like a nail or a screw.

115 **When electricity flows through a wire, it makes a weak magnetic field around it.** If the wire is wrapped into a coil, the magnetism becomes stronger. This is called an electromagnet. Its magnetic force is the same as an ordinary magnet, but when the electricity goes off, the magnetism does too. Some electromagnets are so strong, they can lift whole cars.

▼ The field around a magnet affects objects that contain iron.

Magnetic field
North
South
Magnetic lines of force

QUIZ

Which of these substances or objects is magnetic?
1. Steel spoon 2. Plastic spoon
3. Pencil 4. Drinks can
5. Food can 6. Screwdriver
7. Cooking foil

Answers:
1. Yes 2. No 3. No 4. No 5. Yes 6. Yes 7. No

Electric sparks!

116 Flick a switch and things happen. The television goes off, the computer comes on, lights shine and music plays. Electricity is our favourite form of energy. We send it along wires and plug hundreds of machines into it.

117 Electricity depends on electrons. In certain substances, when electrons are 'pushed', they hop from one atom to the next. When billions do this every second, electricity flows. The 'push' is from a battery or a generator. Electricity only flows in a complete loop or circuit. Break the circuit and the flow stops.

▼ When an electric current flows, the electrons (small blue balls) all move the same way, jumping from one atom to the next. (The red balls are the centres or nuclei of the atoms.)

▼ Solar panels contain many hundreds of fingernail-sized PV (photovoltaic) cells. These convert light energy ('photo') to electrical energy ('voltaic').

▼ A battery has a chemical paste inside its metal casing.

Positive contact

Negative contact on base

118 A battery makes electricity from chemicals. Two different chemicals next to each other, such as an acid and a metal, swap electrons and get the flow going. Electricity's pushing strength is measured in volts. Most batteries are about 1.5, 3, 6 or 9 volts, with 12 volts in cars.

119 Electricity flows easily through some substances, including water and metals. These are electrical conductors. Other substances do not allow electricity to flow. They are insulators. Insulators include wood, plastic, glass, card and ceramics. Metal wires and cables have coverings of plastic, to stop the electricity leaking away.

SCIENCE

120 **Electricity from power stations is carried along cables on high pylons, or buried underground.** This is known as the distribution grid. At thousands of volts, this electricity is extremely dangerous. For use in the home, it is changed to 220 volts (in the UK).

▼ Electricity generators are housed in huge casings, some bigger than trucks.

Pylon holds cables off the ground

◄ To check and repair high-voltage cables, the electricity must be turned off well in advance.

122 **Most of our electricity comes from burning coal, oil, and gas.** Burning them causes pollution, and supplies will eventually run out. So more people are using cleaner renewable energy sources such as solar, wind and water to produce electricity.

121 **Mains electricity is made at a power station.** A fuel such as coal or oil is burned to heat water into high-pressure steam. The steam pushes past the blades of a turbine and makes them spin. The turbines turn generators, which have wire coils near powerful magnets, and the spinning motion makes electricity flow in the coils.

I DON'T BELIEVE IT!
Coal, oil and gas are known as fossil fuels, because they come from the remains of animals and plants that lived long ago.

Compu-science

123 **Computers are amazing machines, but they have to be told exactly what to do.** So we put in instructions and information, by various means. These include typing on a keyboard, inserting a disc or memory stick, downloading from the Internet, using a joystick or games controller, or linking up a camera, scanner or another computer.

124 **Most computers are controlled by instructions from a keyboard and a mouse or touchpad.** The mouse or touchpad moves a cursor around on the screen. You can scroll up, down and sideways by moving your finger and select by tapping or pressing the buttons.

Flat screen monitor

USB (Universal Serial Bus) sockets

External monitor (screen) socket

Headphone socket

Silicon 'wafer'

Plastic casing

◀ This close up of a slice of silicon 'wafer' shows the tiny parts that receive and send information in a computer.

Wire 'feet' link to other part in the computer

125 **Some computers are controlled by talking to them.** They pick up the sounds using a microphone. This is speech recognition technology.

126 **The main brain of a computer is its Central Processing Unit.** It is usually a microchip – millions of electronic parts on a chip of silicon, hardly larger than a fingernail. It receives information and instructions from other microchips, carries out the work, and sends back the results.

SCIENCE

▲ Launched in 2010, the Apple iPad began a new trend in computerized devices called tablets.

127 **Information and instructions are contained in the computer in memory microchips.** There are two kinds. Random Access Memory is like a jotting pad. It keeps changing as the computer carries out its tasks. Read Only Memory is like an instruction book. It usually contains the instructions for how the computer starts up and how all the microchips work together.

▼ The keys on a keyboard have bendy metal contacts that come together when pressed, allowing electricity to flow.

Top flexible layer

Finger presses down on keypad

Conductive strips (red) not touching – circuit is open (incomplete)

Conductive strips make contact and complete circuit

Touchpad

Keyboard

▲ As well as desktop computers, there are also laptops with a fold-up LCD (liquid crystal display) screen.

128 **A computer usually displays its progress on a monitor screen.** It feeds information to output devices such as printers, loudspeakers and robot arms. Information can be stored on memory sticks (chips) or external HDs (hard drive discs), or by uploading it to the Internet.

QUIZ

You may have heard of these sets of letters. Do you know what they mean? Their full written-out versions are all here on these two pages.

1. RAM 2. ROM
3. CPU

Answers:
1. Random Access Memory
2. Read Only Memory
3. Central Processing Unit

57

Pure science

129 The world seems to be made of millions of different substances — such as soil, wood, concrete, plastics and air. These are combinations of simpler substances. If you could take them apart, you would see that they are made of pure substances called elements.

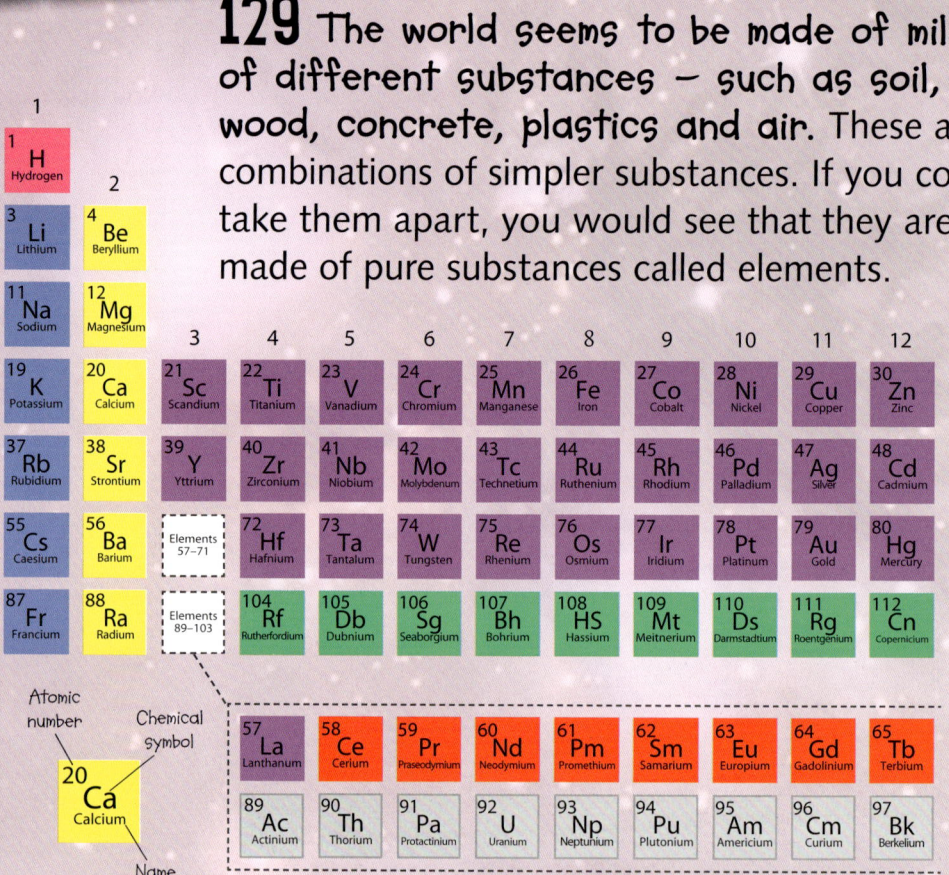

▶ Stars are made mainly of burning hydrogen, which is why they are so hot and bright.

▲ The Periodic Table is a chart of all the elements. In each row the atoms get heavier from left to right. Each column (up-down) contains elements with similar chemical features. Every element has a chemical symbol, name, and atomic number, which is the number of particles called protons in its central part, or nucleus.

130 Hydrogen is the simplest element and it is the first in the Periodic Table. This means it has the smallest atoms. It is a very light gas, which floats upwards in air. Hydrogen was used to fill giant airships. But there was a problem — hydrogen catches fire easily and explodes.

131 About 90 elements are found naturally on and in the Earth. In an element, all of its particles, called atoms, are exactly the same as each other. Just as important, they are all different from the atoms of any other element.

Element types
- Alkali metals
- Alkaline metals
- Transition metals
- Other metals
- Other non-metals
- Halogens
- Inert gases
- Lanthanides
- Actinides
- Trans-actinides

Note: Elements 113–118 are synthetic elements that have only been created briefly, so their properties cannot be known for certain.

QUIZ
1. How many elements are found naturally on Earth?
2. Which lightweight metal is very useful?
3. Which element makes up stars?
4. What do diamonds and coal have in common?

Answers:
1. About 90 2. Aluminium 3. Hydrogen 4. They are both made of pure carbon

133 Uranium is a heavy and dangerous element. It gives off harmful rays and tiny particles. This process is called radioactivity and it can cause sickness, burns and diseases such as cancer. Radioactivity is a form of energy and, under careful control, radioactive elements are used as fuel in nuclear power stations.

▶ Aluminium is a strong but light metal that is ideal for forming the body of vehicles such as planes.

132 Carbon is a very important element in living things — including our own bodies. It joins easily with atoms of other elements to make large groups of atoms called molecules. When it is pure, carbon can be two different forms. These are soft, powdery soot, and hard, glittering diamond. The form depends on how the carbon atoms join to each other.

Bond (link) Atom

134 Aluminium is an element that is a metal, and it is one of the most useful in modern life. It is light and strong, it does not rust, and it is resistant to corrosion. Saucepans, drinks cans, cooking foil and jet planes are made mainly of aluminium.

◀ Diamond is a form of the element carbon where the atoms are linked, or bonded, in a very strong box-like pattern.

On the body's outside

135 **Your skin is amazing!** Its surface is made of tiny cells that have filled up with a hard, tough substance called keratin, and then died. So when you look at a human body, most of what you see is 'dead'! You are continuously shedding dead skin cells.

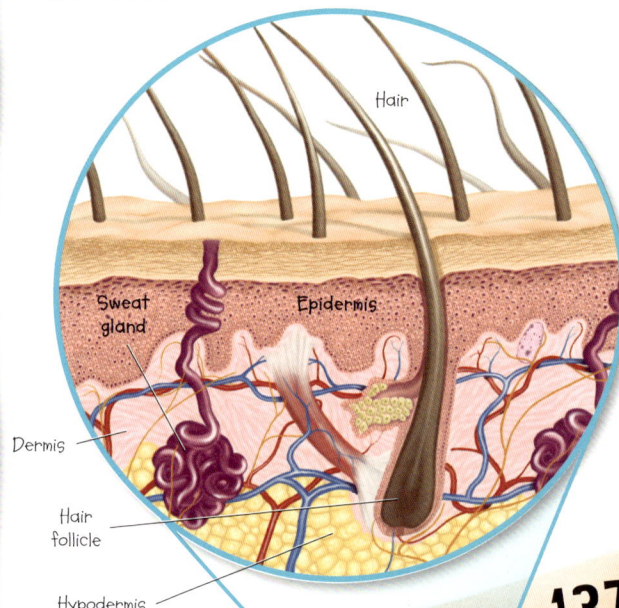

136 **Skin rubs off all the time, and grows all the time too.** Just under the surface, living cells make more new cells that gradually fill with keratin, die and move up to the surface. It takes about four weeks from a new skin cell being made to when it reaches the surface and is rubbed off. This upper layer of skin is called the epidermis.

▲ Although your skin is just 2 millimetres thick on average, it is so important that it receives up to one third of your body's blood supply.

137 **The lower layer, the dermis, is thicker than the epidermis.** It is made of tiny, bendy, thread-like fibres of the substance collagen. The dermis also contains small blood vessels, tiny sweat glands, and micro-sensors that detect touch. The innermost layer is mostly fat, and is called the hypodermis.

▲ Your skin is waterproof, and gives you some protection against the harmful effects of sunlight. It even helps to nourish you by using sunlight to make vitamin D.

SCIENCE

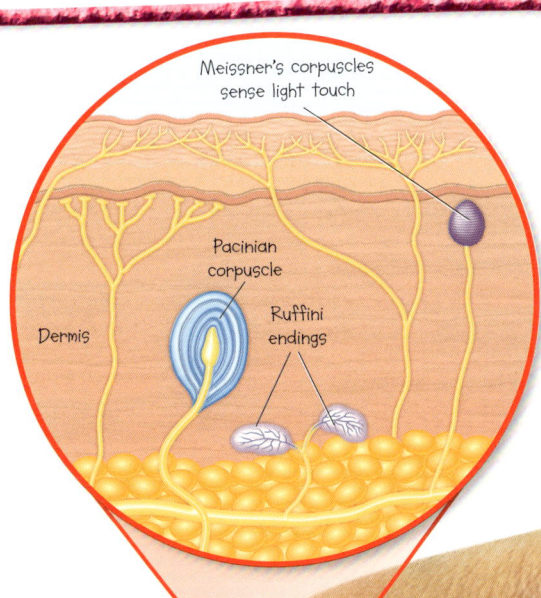

138 One of skin's important jobs is to protect the body. It stops the delicate inner parts from being rubbed, knocked or scraped. Skin also prevents body fluids from leaking away and it keeps out dirt and germs, preventing infection.

◀ Some sensors, called Pacinian corpuscles, respond quickly to pressure and then stop. Others, called Ruffini endings, respond slowly then keep going.

139 Skin gives us our sense of touch. Millions of microscopic sensors in the lower layer of skin, the dermis, are joined by nerves to the brain. These sensors detect different kinds of touch, from a light stroke to heavy pressure, heat or cold, and movement. Pain sensors detect when skin is damaged. Ouch!

140 Your skin helps to keep your body at the same temperature. If you become too hot, it releases sweat, which draws heat from the body as it dries. Also, the blood vessels in the lower layer of skin widen, to lose more heat through the skin. This is why a hot person looks sweaty and red in the face.

The bony body

141 **Without bones, the body would be as soft as a jellyfish!** Your bones form a strong but light framework called the skeleton. Bones do many jobs. The long bones in the arms work like levers to reach out the hands. The finger bones grasp and grip. Bones also protect the body's organs. The skull protects the brain and the ribs shield the lungs and heart.

142 **The skeleton is strong and rigid, yet can bend pretty much any way you want.** That's because it's made of lots of separate bones linked only by movable joints. Here, the bones are held together by fibres called ligaments and cushioned by smooth, rubbery cartilage.

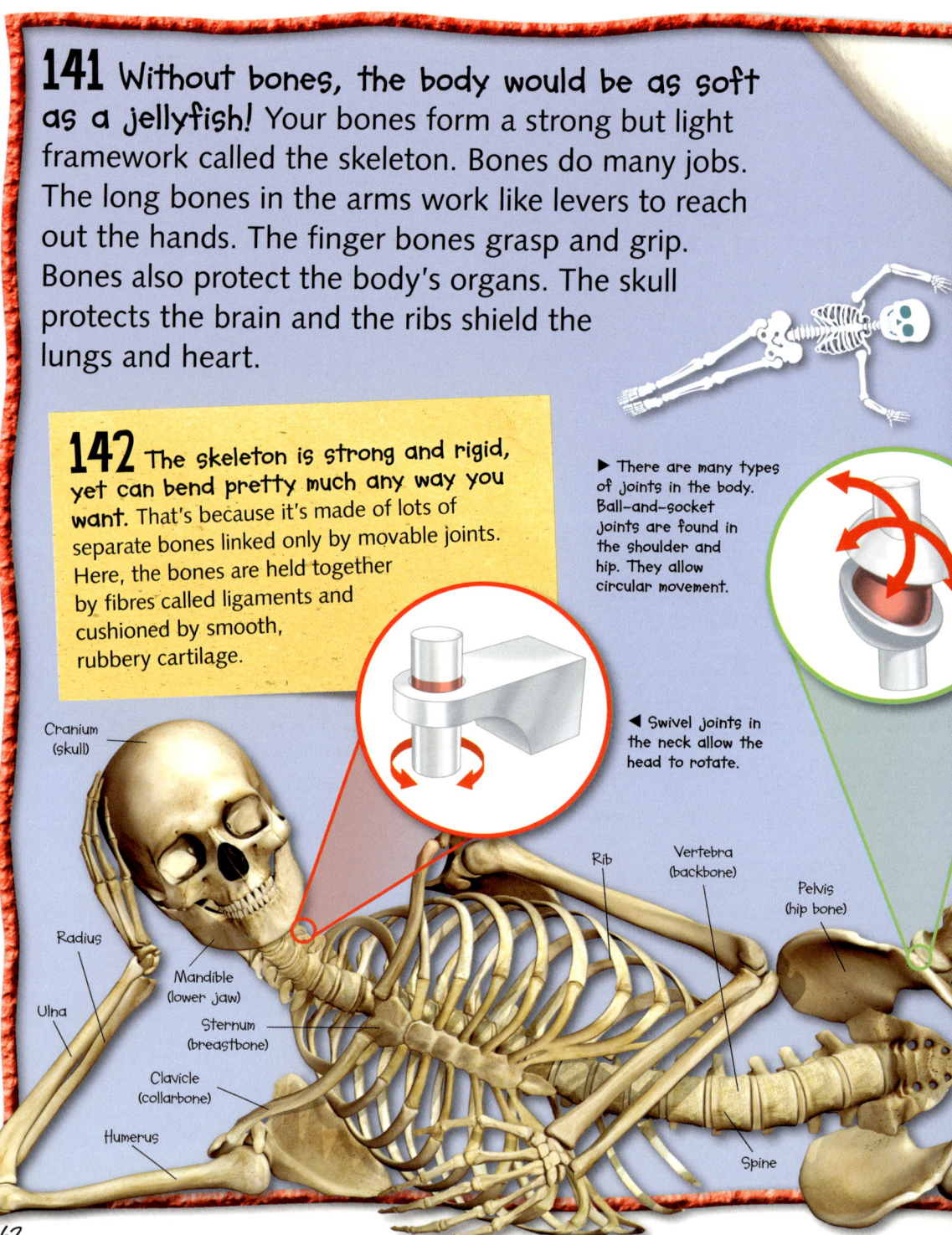

▶ There are many types of joints in the body. Ball-and-socket joints are found in the shoulder and hip. They allow circular movement.

◀ Swivel joints in the neck allow the head to rotate.

Cranium (skull)
Radius
Ulna
Mandible (lower jaw)
Sternum (breastbone)
Clavicle (collarbone)
Humerus
Rib
Vertebra (backbone)
Pelvis (hip bone)
Spine

SCIENCE

143 Bone contains threads of a tough, slightly bendy substance called collagen. It also has hard minerals such as calcium and phosphate. Together, the collagen and minerals make a bone strong and rigid, yet able to bend slightly under stress. Bones have blood vessels for nourishment and nerves to feel pressure and pain. In the middle, bones contain a jelly-like substance called marrow. The marrow of the breastbone, ribs and hips produces new blood cells.

▲ Bone has a hard layer outside, a spongy layer next, and soft marrow in the middle.

◀ Hinge joints, like those in the knee, allow a swinging movement to and fro.

144 All the bones together make up the skeleton. Most people have 206 bones, from head to toe as follows:
- 8 in the upper part of the skull, the cranium or braincase
- 14 in the face
- 6 tiny ear bones, 3 deep in each ear
- 1 in the neck, which is floating and not directly connected to any other bone
- 26 in the spinal column or backbone
- 25 in the chest, being 24 ribs and the breastbone
- 32 in each arm, from shoulder to fingertips (8 in each wrist)
- 31 in each leg, from hip to toetips (7 in each ankle)

▼ Many of the bones in your body are long and thin. Exceptions include the pelvis and the skull.

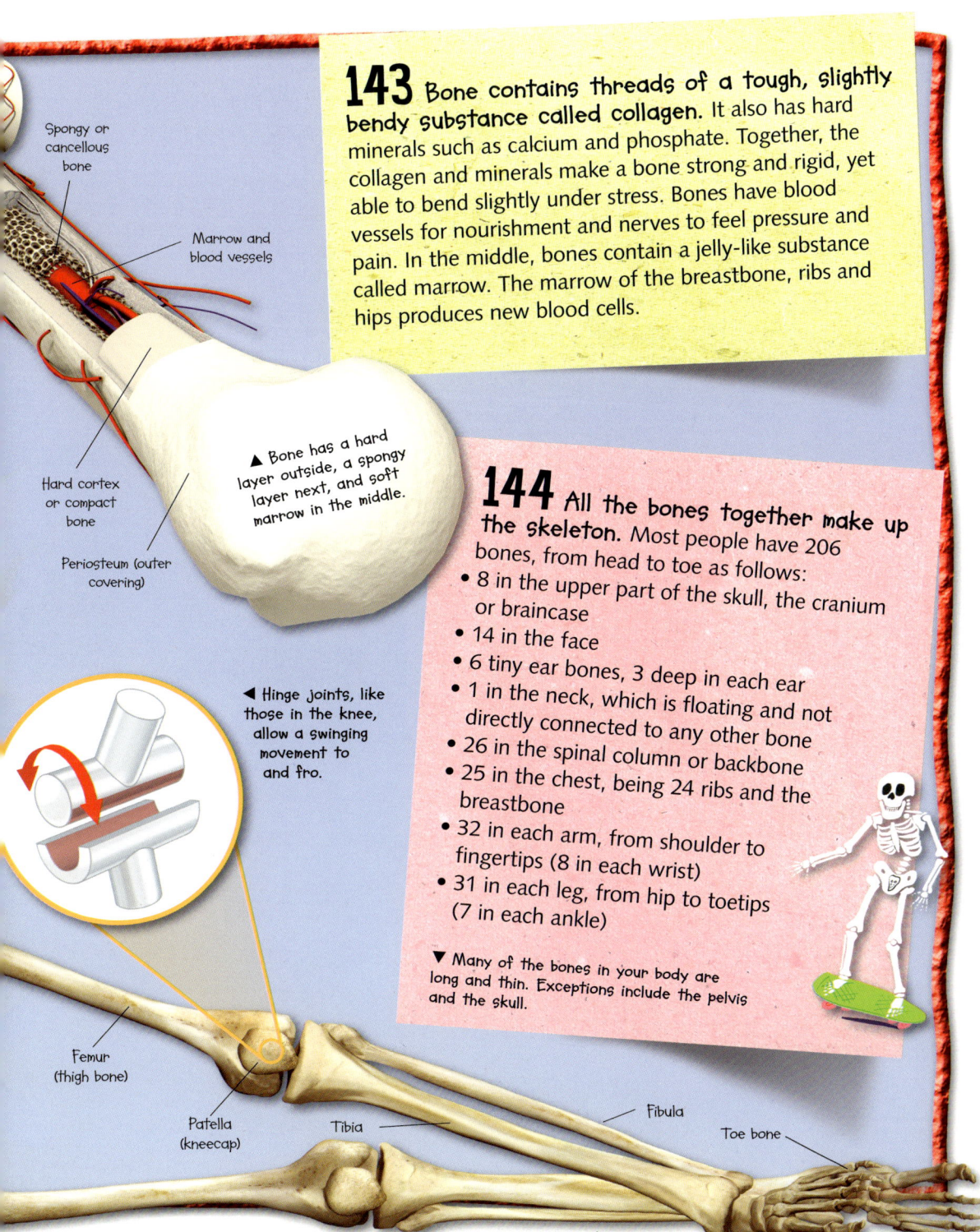

When muscles pull

145 **Every move you make depends on muscles.** You have two main kinds of muscles. Skeletal (voluntary) muscles cover your skeleton and allow you to move. Involuntary muscles work automatically to control body functions, such as your heartbeat.

146 You have 640 skeletal muscles. Some are wide or broad, and shaped like flat sheets or triangles. These include the three layers of muscles in the lower front and sides of the body, called the abdominal wall muscles. If you tense or contract them, they pull your tummy in.

147 **A muscle is joined to a bone by its tendon.** This is where the end of the muscle becomes slimmer or tapers, and is strengthened by strong, thick fibres of collagen. The fibres are fixed firmly into the surface of the bone.

I DON'T BELIEVE IT!

It's easier to smile than to frown. There are about 40 muscles under the skin of the face. You use almost all of these to make a deep frown, but only about half of them to show a broad grin.

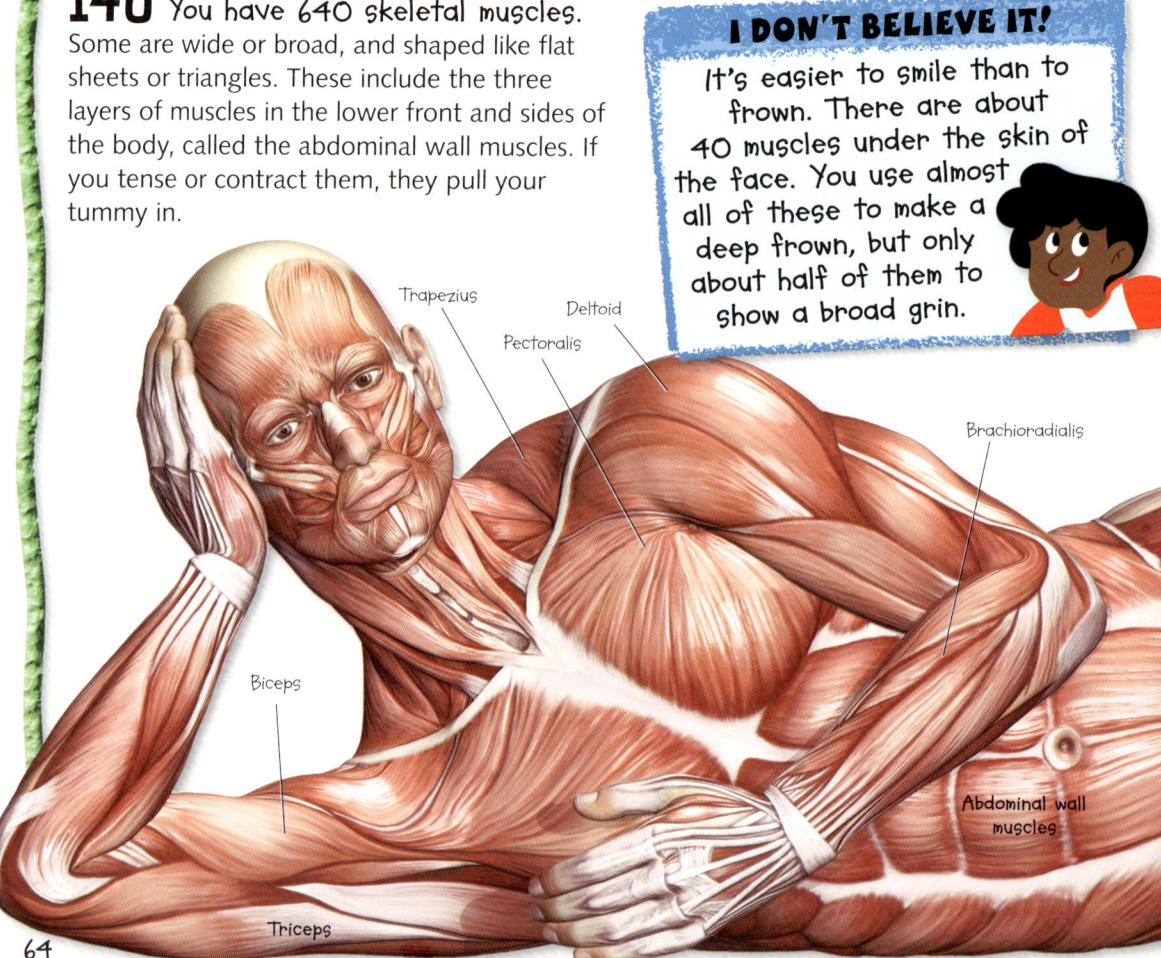

Trapezius, Deltoid, Pectoralis, Brachioradialis, Biceps, Abdominal wall muscles, Triceps

SCIENCE

148 Most muscles are long and slim, and joined to bones at each end. As they contract they pull on the bones and move them. As this happens, the muscle becomes wider, or more bulging in the middle. To move the bone back again, a muscle on the other side of it contracts, while the first muscle relaxes and is pulled back to its original length.

◀ The biceps and triceps muscles in your upper arm work in conjunction to pull your forearm one way then the other.

149 Every muscle in the body has a scientific or medical name, which is often quite long and complicated. Some of these names are familiar to people who do exercise and sports. The 'pecs' are the pectoralis major muscles across the chest. The 'biceps' are the biceps brachii muscles in the upper arms, which bulge when you bend your elbow.

150 If you take plenty of exercise or play sport, you do not gain new muscles. But the muscles you have become larger and stronger. This keeps them healthy. Muscles which are not used much may become weak and floppy.

▼ The muscles shown here are some of those just beneath the skin, called superficial muscles. Under them is another layer, the deep muscle layer. In some areas there is an additional layer, the medial muscles.

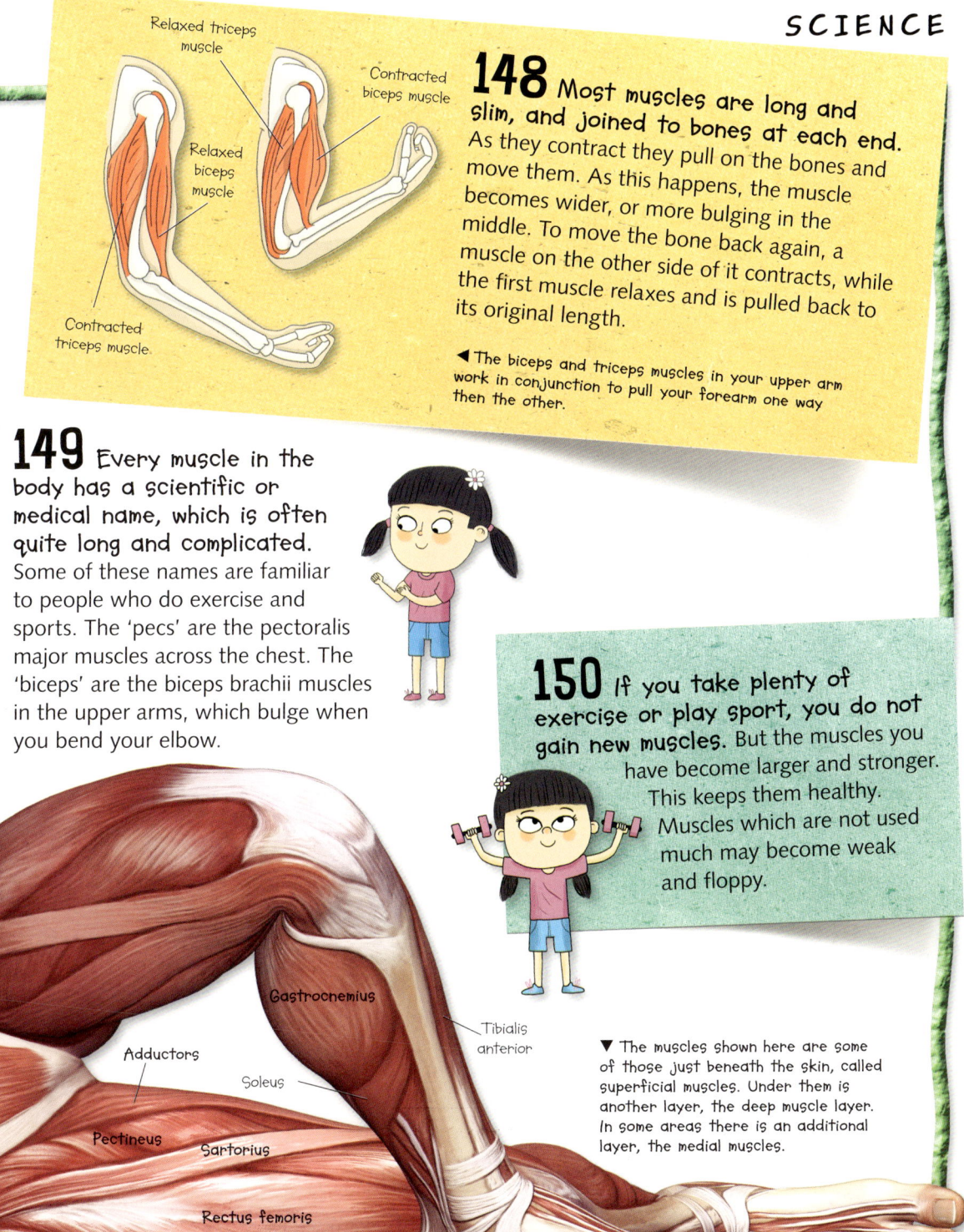

Breathing parts

151 The main parts of the respiratory (breathing) system are the two lungs in the chest. Each one is shaped like a tall cone, with the pointed end at shoulder level.

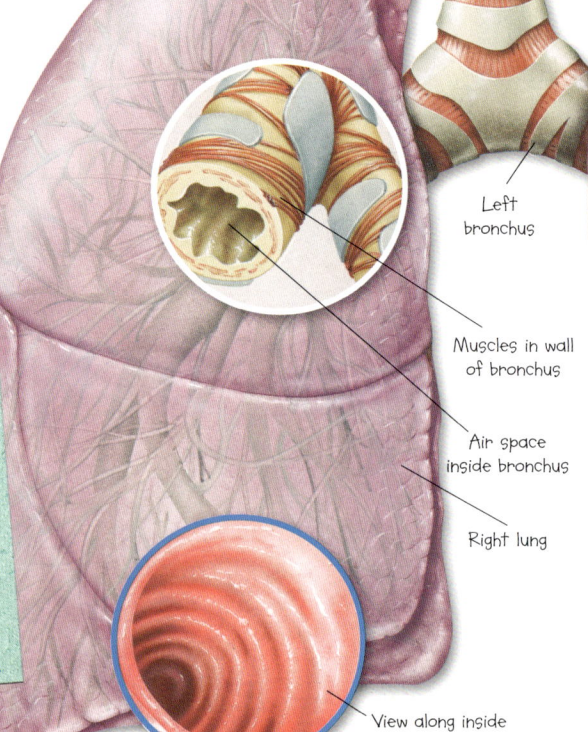

Windpipe

Left bronchus

Muscles in wall of bronchus

Air space inside bronchus

Right lung

View along inside of bronchus

152 Air comes in and out of the lungs along the windpipe, which branches at its base to form two main air tubes, the bronchi. One goes to each lung. Inside the lung, each bronchus branches into tens of thousands of narrower air tubes, called bronchioles. At the end of each bronchiole are groups of tiny 'bubbles' called alveoli.

I DON'T BELIEVE IT!
On average, the air breathed in and out through the night by a sleeping person would fill an average-sized bedroom. This is why some people like to sleep with the door or window open!

153 There are more than 200 million alveoli in each lung. Oxygen from breathed-in air passes through the very thin linings of the alveoli to equally tiny blood vessels on the other side. The blood carries the oxygen away, around the body. At the same time a waste substance, carbon dioxide, seeps through the blood vessel, into the alveoli. As you breathe out, the lungs blow out the carbon dioxide.

SCIENCE

◀ When you breathe in, your lungs inflate like balloons to draw air in through your nose and mouth and down your windpipe.

154 **Breathing needs muscle power!** The main breathing muscle is the dome-shaped diaphragm at the base of the chest. When you breathe in, it becomes flatter, making the lungs bigger. At the same time, rib muscles lift the ribs, also making the lungs bigger. When you breathe out, the diaphragm and rib muscles relax. The stretched lungs spring back like a deflated balloon and blow out stale air.

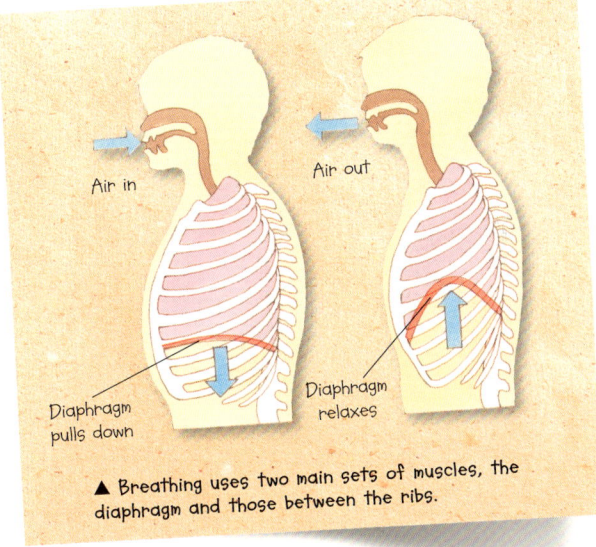

▲ Breathing uses two main sets of muscles, the diaphragm and those between the ribs.

Bronchiole
Blood vessels
Bunch of alveoli

◀ The alveoli are like a bunch of tiny balloons that inflate and deflate with every breath you take.

Air space in alveoli

155 As you rest or sleep, each breath sends about half a litre of air in and out, 15 to 20 times each minute. After great activity, such as running a race, the body needs to replace the oxygen used by the muscles for energy. So you take deeper breaths faster – 3 litres or more of air, 50 times or more each minute.

67

Bite, chew, gulp

156 **The hardest parts of your whole body are the ones that make holes in your food — teeth.** They have a covering of whitish or yellowish enamel, which is stronger than most kinds of rocks! Teeth need to last a lifetime of biting, nibbling, gnashing, munching and chewing. They are your own food processors.

157 **There are four main shapes of teeth.** The front ones are incisors, and each has a straight, sharp edge, like a spade or chisel, to cut through food. Next are canines, which are taller and more pointed, used mainly for tearing and pulling. Behind them are premolars and molars, which are lower and flatter with small bumps, for crushing and grinding.

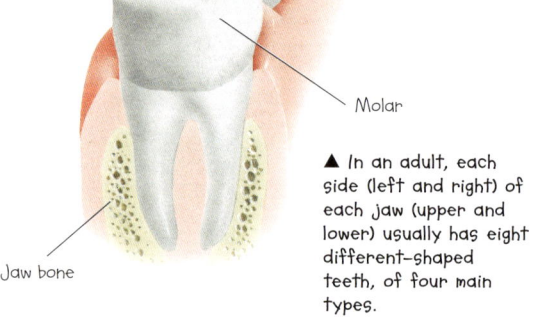

▲ In an adult, each side (left and right) of each jaw (upper and lower) usually has eight different-shaped teeth, of four main types.

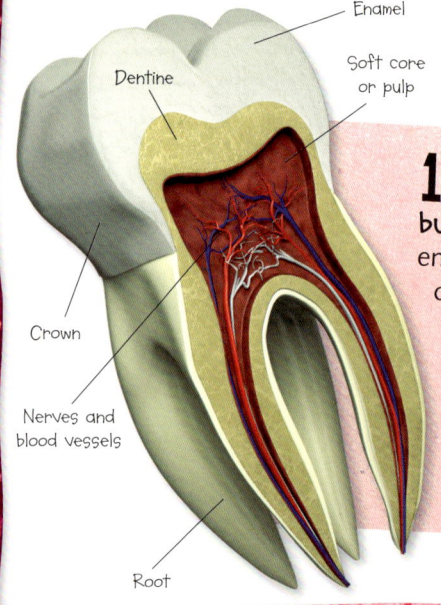

◀ At the centre of a tooth is living pulp, with many blood vessels and nerve endings that pass into the jaw bone.

158 **A tooth may look almost dead, but it is very much alive.** Under the enamel is slightly softer dentine. In the middle of the tooth is the dental pulp. This has blood vessels to nourish the whole tooth, and nerves that feel pressure, heat, cold and pain. The lower part of the tooth, strongly fixed in the jaw bone, is the root. The enamel-covered part above the gum is the crown.

SCIENCE

159 Teeth are very strong and tough, but they do need to be cleaned properly and regularly. Germs called bacteria live on old bits of food in the mouth. They make waste products which are acidic and eat into the enamel and dentine, causing holes called cavities. Which do you prefer – cleaning your teeth after main meals and before bedtime, or the agony of toothache?

▶ Clean your teeth by brushing in different directions and then flossing between them. They will stay healthier for longer.

160 Teeth are designed to last a lifetime. Well, not quite, because the body has two sets. There are 20 small teeth in the first or baby set. The first ones usually appear above the gum by about six months of age, the last ones at three years old. As you and your mouth grow, the baby teeth fall out from about seven years old. They are replaced by 32 larger teeth in the adult set.

◀ The first set of teeth lasts about ten years, while the second set can last ten times longer.

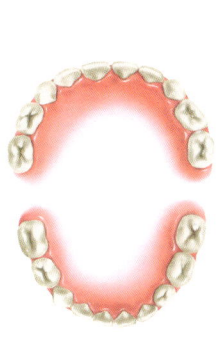

First set
(milk or deciduous teeth)

Second set
(adult or permanent set)

161 After chewing, food is swallowed into the gullet (oesophagus). This pushes the food powerfully down through the chest, past the heart and lungs, into the stomach.

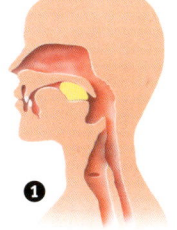

❶ Tongue pushes food to the back of the throat

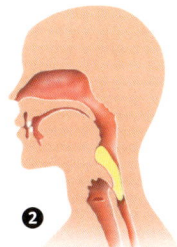

❷ Throat muscles squeeze the food downwards

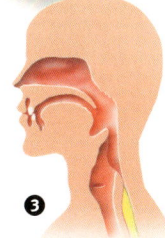

❸ The oesophagus pushes food to the stomach

Food's long journey

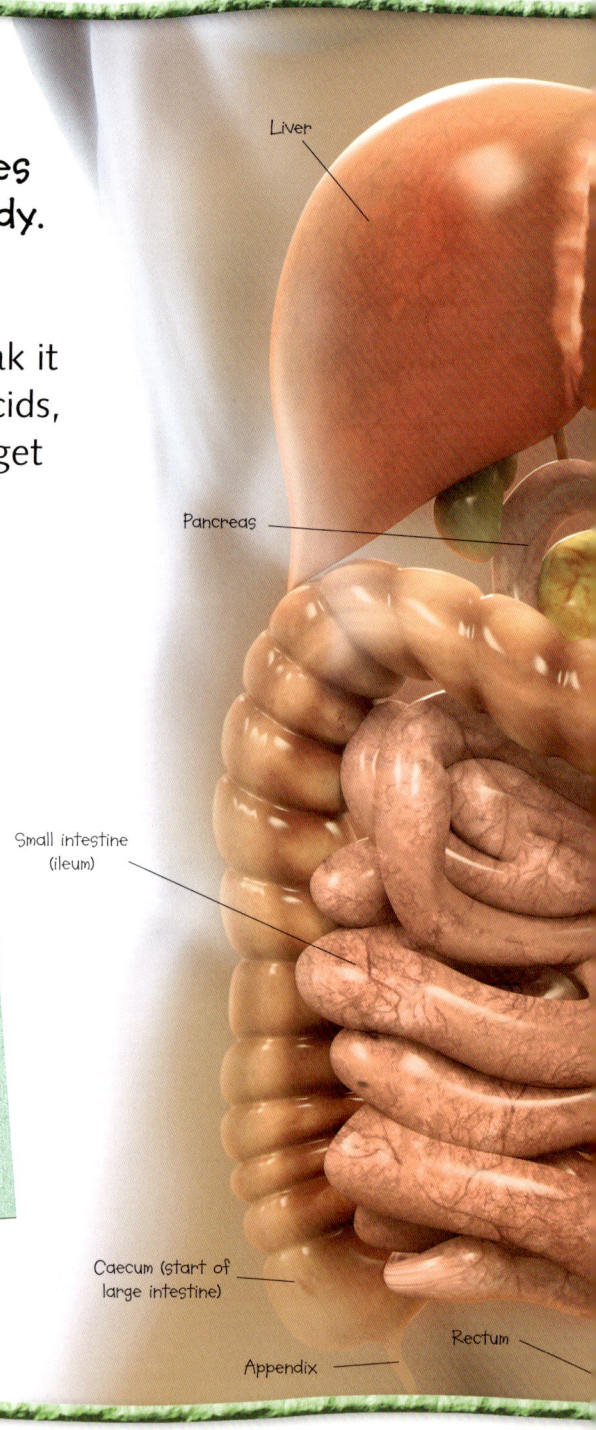

162 The digestive system is like a tunnel about 9 metres long, through the body. It includes parts of the body that bite food, chew it, swallow it, churn it up and break it down with natural juices and acids, take in its goodness, and then get rid of the leftovers.

163 The stomach is a bag with strong, muscular walls. It stretches as it fills with food and drink, and its lining makes powerful digestive acids and juices called enzymes, to attack the food. The muscles in its walls squirm and squeeze to mix the food and juices.

164 Over a few hours, the stomach digests food and mashes it into a thick pulp. This oozes into the small intestine, which is only 4 centimetres wide but more than 5 metres long. It absorbs nutrients and useful substances through its lining, into the body.

▶ The digestive parts almost fill the lower part of the main body, called the abdomen.

SCIENCE

165 **Any indigestible food passes on into the large intestine.** It is wider than the small intestine but much shorter, only 1.5 metres. It takes in fluids and more nutrients from the food, and then squashes what's left into lumps, ready to leave the body.

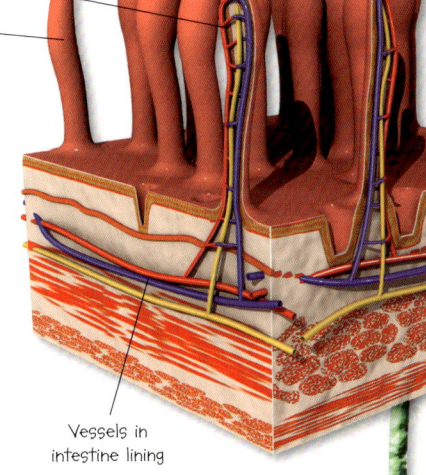

Stomach

Large intestine

Vessels inside villus

Villus

▶ The lining of the small intestine has thousands of tiny finger-like parts called villi, which take nutrients from food into the blood and lymph system.

Vessels in intestine lining

166 **The liver and pancreas are also parts of the digestive system.** The liver sorts out and changes the many nutrients from digestion, and stores some of them. The pancreas makes powerful digestive juices that pass to the small intestine to break down the food.

167 **What's in the leftovers?** The lumps, called faeces, consist of about one-half undigested food. Some of the rest is rubbed-off parts of the stomach and intestine lining. The rest is millions of 'friendly' but dead microbes (bacteria) from the intestine. They help to digest our food for us, and in return we give them a warm, food-filled place to live. The faeces passes into the rectum to leave the body.

I DON'T BELIEVE IT!

Your stomach produces hydrochloric acid strong enough to dissolve a lump of bone in a few hours. That's why your stomach lining is coated with protective mucus.

Blood in the body

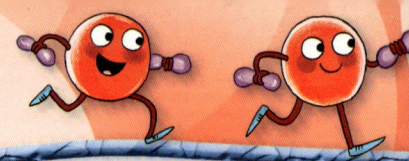

168 **The heart beats to pump blood all around the body and pass its vital oxygen and nutrients to every part.** The same blood goes round and round, or circulates, in its network of blood vessels. So the heart, blood vessels and blood are known as the circulatory system.

◀ Blood vessels divide, or branch, to reach every body part.

▶ There are three main kinds of blood vessels.

169 **Blood travels from the heart through strong, thick-walled vessels called arteries.** These divide again and again, becoming smaller until they form tiny vessels narrower than hairs, called capillaries. Oxygen and nutrients seep from the blood through the thin capillary walls to the body parts around. At the same time, carbon dioxide and waste substances seep from body parts into the blood, to be carried away. Capillaries join again and again to form wide vessels called veins, which take blood back to the heart.

170 **In addition to delivering oxygen and nutrients, and carrying away carbon dioxide and waste, blood has many other vital tasks.** It carries body control substances called hormones. It spreads heat evenly around the body from busy, warmer parts such as the heart, liver and muscles. It forms a sticky clot to seal a cut and it carries substances that attack germs and other tiny invaders.

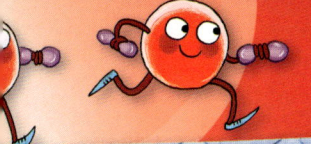

SCIENCE

171 **Blood has four main parts.** The largest is billions of tiny, saucer-shaped red cells, which make up almost half of the total volume of blood and carry oxygen. Second is the white cells, which clean the blood, prevent disease and fight germs. The third part is billions of tiny platelets, which help blood to clot. Fourth is watery plasma, in which the other parts float.

QUIZ

Can you match these blood parts with their descriptions?
a. White blood cell
b. Red blood cell   c. Platelet
1. Oxygen-carrying part of the blood
2. Part that helps blood to clot
3. Germ-fighting part of the blood

Answers:
a3 b1 c2

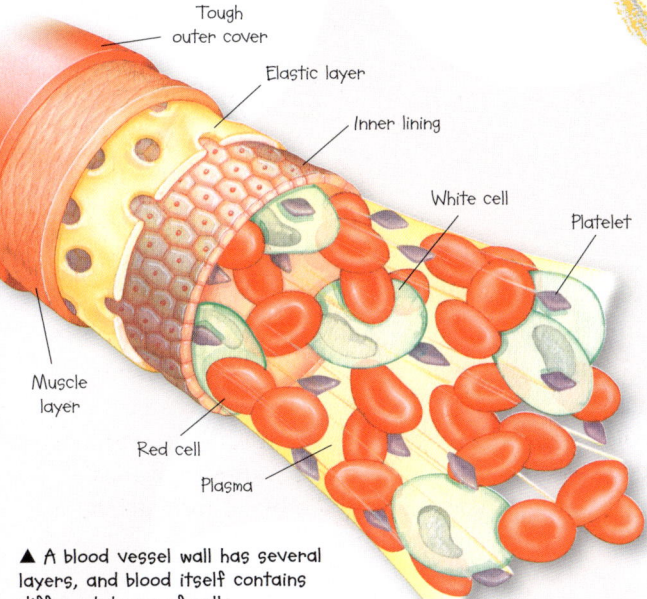

▲ A blood vessel wall has several layers, and blood itself contains different types of cells.

▼ Each kidney has about one million tiny filters, called nephrons, in its outer layer, or cortex.

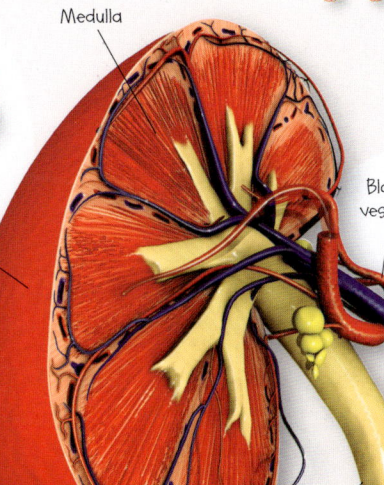

172 **Blood is cleaned by two kidneys, situated in the middle of your back.** They filter the blood and make a liquid called urine, which contains unwanted and waste substances, plus excess or 'spare' water. The urine trickles from each kidney down a tube, the ureter, into a stretchy bag, the bladder. It's stored here until you can get rid of it – at your convenience.

73

The beating body

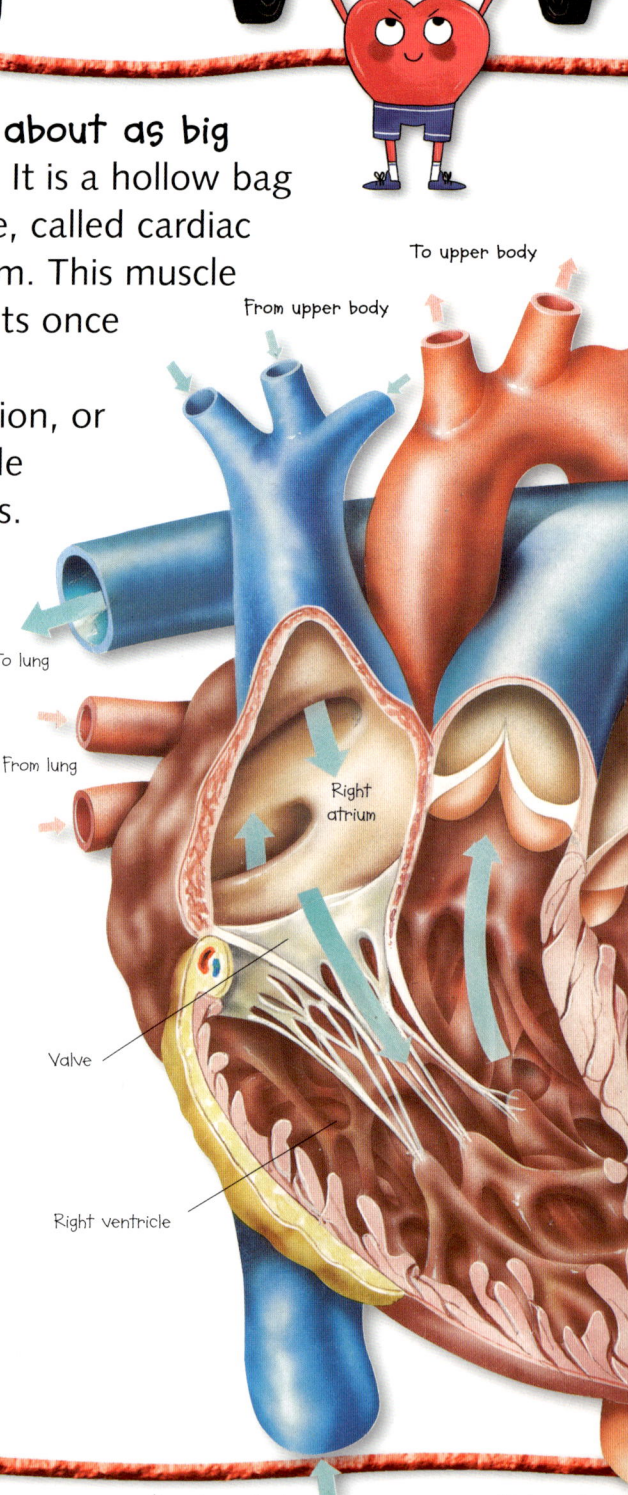

173 **The heart is about as big as a clenched fist.** It is a hollow bag of very strong muscle, called cardiac muscle or myocardium. This muscle never tires. It contracts once every second or more often, throughout life. The contraction, or heartbeat, pumps blood inside the heart out into the arteries. As the heart relaxes it fills again with blood from the veins.

174 **Inside, the heart is not one bag-like pump, but two pumps side by side.** The left pump sends blood all around the body, from head to toe, to deliver its oxygen (systemic circulation). The blood comes back to the right pump and is sent to the lungs, to collect more oxygen (pulmonary circulation). The blood returns to the left pump and starts the whole journey again.

▶ The heart is two pumps side by side, and each pump has two chambers, the upper atrium and the lower ventricle.

SCIENCE

175 **Inside the heart are four sets of bendy flaps called valves.** These open to let blood flow the right way. If the blood tries to move the wrong way, it pushes the flaps together and the valve closes. Valves make sure the blood flows the correct way, rather than sloshing to and fro, in and out of the heart, with each beat.

176 **The heart is the body's most active part, and it needs plenty of energy brought by the blood.** The blood flows through small vessels, which branch across its surface and down into its thick walls. These are called the coronary vessels.

Aorta (main artery)

Pulmonary artery to lung

177 **The heart beats at different rates, depending on what the body is doing.** When the muscles are active they need more energy and oxygen, brought by the blood. So the heart beats faster, 120 times each minute or more. At rest, the heart slows to 60 to 80 beats per minute.

▶ This X-ray of a chest shows a pacemaker that has been implanted to control an irregular heartbeat.

178 **Special cells in the heart send out electrical signals.** These make your heart beat at a steady rate. If these signals aren't working, a doctor may fit a device called a pacemaker to correct it.

▶ Doctors use ECG machines to monitor the electrical activity of the heart.

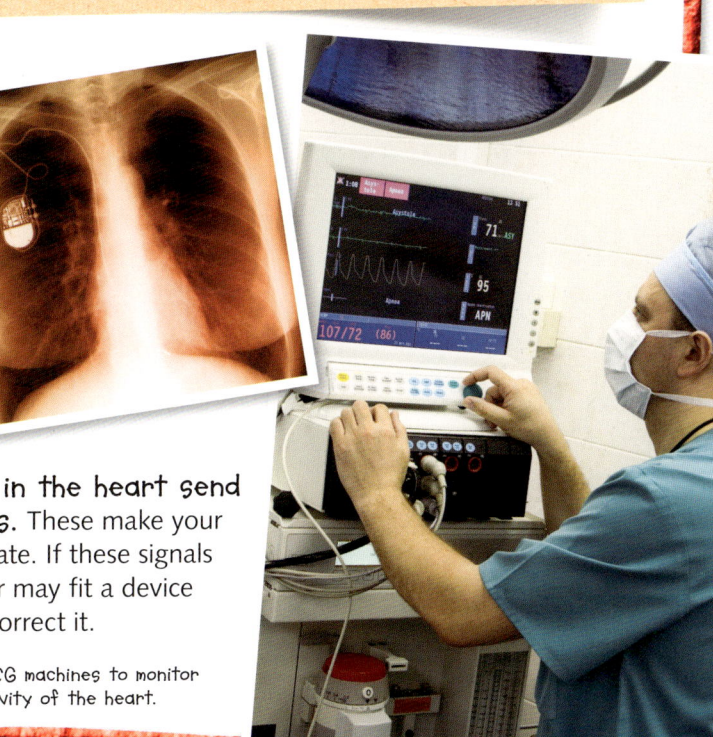

Looking and listening

179 **The body finds out about the world around it by its senses.** Your eyes detect the brightness, colours and patterns of light rays, and change these into patterns of nerve signals that they send to the brain. More than half of the knowledge, information and memories stored in the brain come into the body through the eyes.

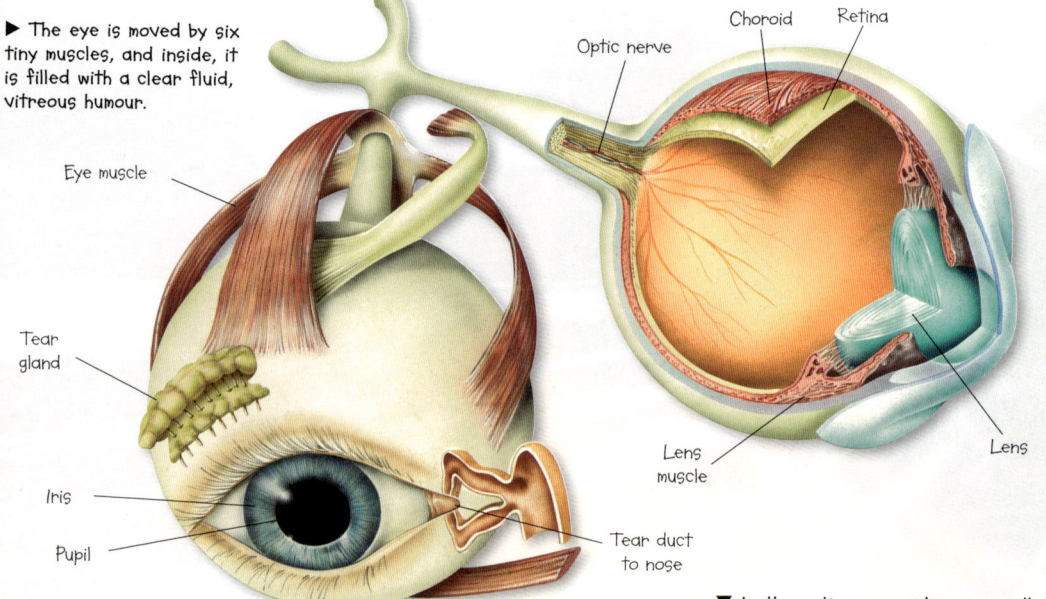

▶ The eye is moved by six tiny muscles, and inside, it is filled with a clear fluid, vitreous humour.

180 **Each eye is a ball about 2.5 centimetres across.** At the front is a clear dome, the cornea, which lets light through a small, dark-looking hole just behind it, the pupil. The light then passes through a pea-shaped lens, which bends the rays so they shine a clear picture onto the inside back of the eye, the retina. This has 125 million tiny cells, rods and cones, which detect the light and make nerve signals to send along the optic nerve to the brain.

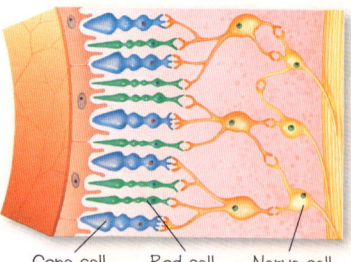

▼ In the retina are wider cone cells, narrower rod cells, and many nerve cells with long fibres connecting them.

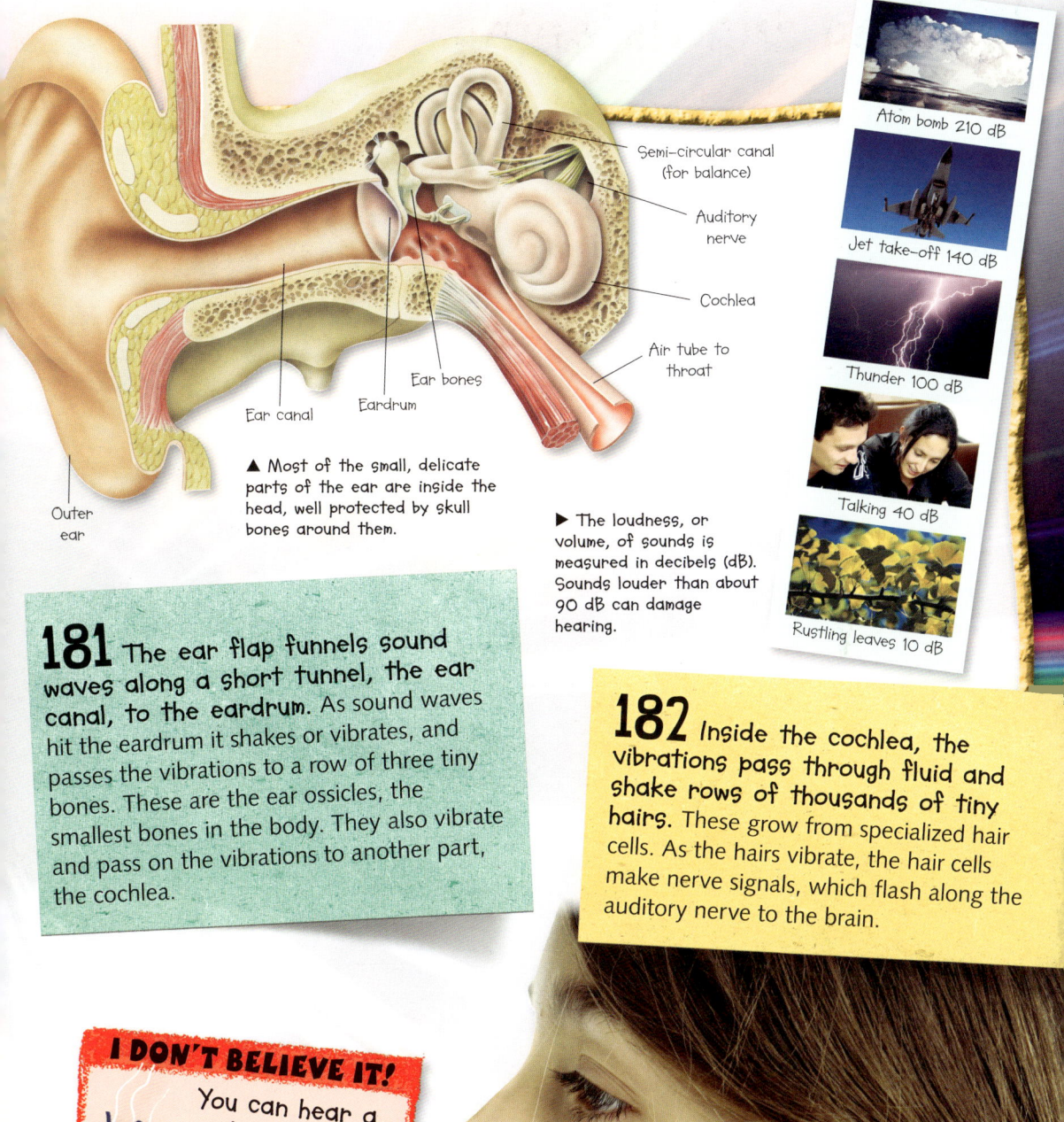

▲ Most of the small, delicate parts of the ear are inside the head, well protected by skull bones around them.

▶ The loudness, or volume, of sounds is measured in decibels (dB). Sounds louder than about 90 dB can damage hearing.

181 **The ear flap funnels sound waves along a short tunnel, the ear canal, to the eardrum.** As sound waves hit the eardrum it shakes or vibrates, and passes the vibrations to a row of three tiny bones. These are the ear ossicles, the smallest bones in the body. They also vibrate and pass on the vibrations to another part, the cochlea.

182 **Inside the cochlea, the vibrations pass through fluid and shake rows of thousands of tiny hairs.** These grow from specialized hair cells. As the hairs vibrate, the hair cells make nerve signals, which flash along the auditory nerve to the brain.

I DON'T BELIEVE IT!
You can hear a wider range of sounds than an owl, but a narrower range than a cow.

▶ Some people need help to hear properly. A hearing aid worn inside the ear can help them to hear better.

Smelling and tasting

183 You cannot see smells, which are tiny particles floating in the air – but your nose can smell them. Your nose can detect more than 10,000 different scents. Smell is useful because it warns us if food is bad or rotten, and perhaps dangerous to eat. That's why we sniff a new or strange food item before trying it.

184 Smell particles drift with breathed-in air into the nose and through the nasal cavity behind it. At the top of the cavity are two patches of lining, each about the area of a thumbnail and with 5 million olfactory cells. The particles land on their sticky hairs, and if they fit into landing sites called receptors there, like a key into a lock, then nerve signals flash along the olfactory nerve to the brain.

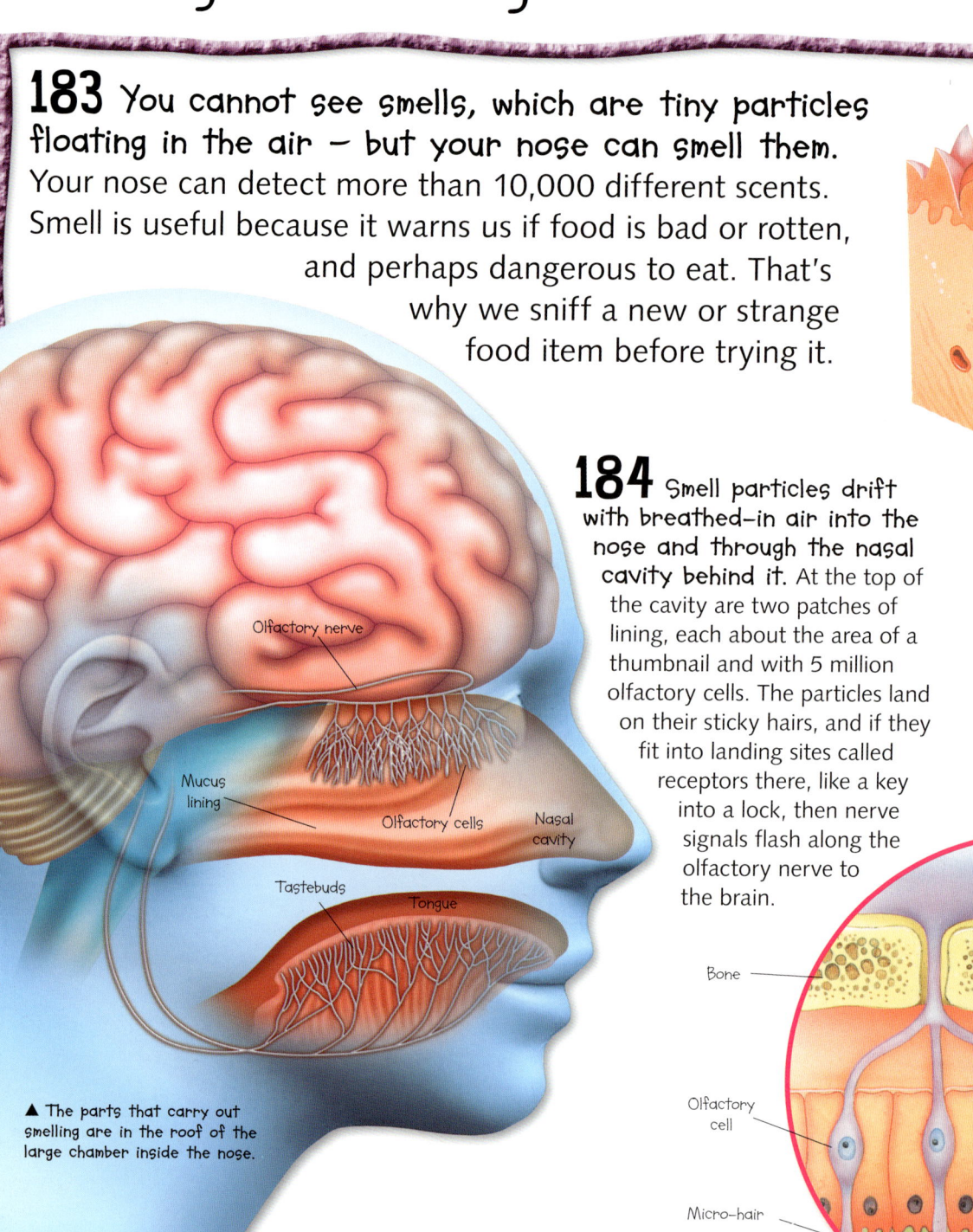

▲ The parts that carry out smelling are in the roof of the large chamber inside the nose.

SCIENCE

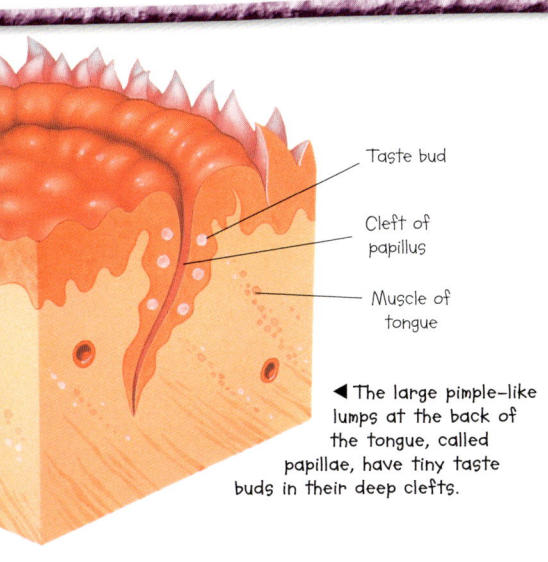

- Taste bud
- Cleft of papillus
- Muscle of tongue

◀ The large pimple-like lumps at the back of the tongue, called papillae, have tiny taste buds in their deep clefts.

186 The body's most flexible muscle is also the one which is coated with 10,000 micro-sensors for taste – the tongue. Each micro-sensor is a taste bud shaped like a tiny onion. Most taste buds are along the tip, sides and rear upper surface of the tongue. They are scattered around the much larger flaps and lumps on the tongue, which are called papillae.

185 Taste works in a similar way to smell, but it detects flavour particles in foods and drinks. The particles touch tiny hairs sticking up from hair cells in the taste buds. If the particles fit into receptors there, then the hair cell makes nerve signals, which go along the facial and other nerves to the brain.

QUIZ

The tongue detects five basic flavours. Which of these foods is sweet, salty, umami (savoury), bitter or sour?
1. Mushroom 2. Lemon
3. Pretzel 4. Kale
5. Strawberry

Answers:
1. umami 2. sour 3. salty 4. bitter 5. sweet

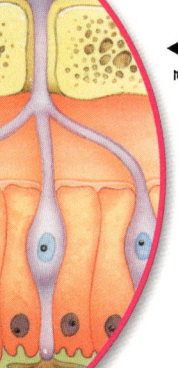

◀ Olfactory (smell) cells have micro-hairs facing down into the nasal cavity, which detect smell particles landing on them.

The nervous body

Brain
Spinal cord
Sciatic nerve
Tibial nerve

187 **The body contains thousands of kilometres of nerves.** These are pale, shiny threads which carry tiny electrical pulses known as nerve signals or neural messages. They form a vast information-sending network that reaches every part, almost like the body's own Internet.

188 Each nerve is a bundle of much thinner parts called nerve fibres. Like wires in a telephone cable, these carry their own tiny electrical nerve signals. A typical nerve signal has a strength of 0.1 volts (one-fifteenth as strong as a torch battery). The slowest nerve signals travel about half a metre each second, the fastest at more than 100 metres per second.

Synapse

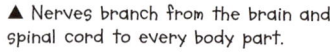
▲ Nerves branch from the brain and spinal cord to every body part.

189 All nerve signals are similar, but there are two main kinds, depending on where they are going. Sensory nerve signals travel from the sensory parts (eyes, ears, nose, tongue and skin) to the brain. Motor nerve signals travel from the brain out to the muscles, to make the body move about.

I DON'T BELIEVE IT!
Eating chocolate sets off floods of neurotransmitters (chemicals) such as endorphins and serotonin. These are linked to happy feelings, which may be why people like chocolate!

SCIENCE

Nerve cell body · **Axon** · **Tip of axon** · **Dendrites** · **Covering of axon (myelin sheath)**

Axon terminal of sending neuron · **Dendrite of receiving neuron** · **Neurotransmitters**

▼ Sports such as skiing cause us to produce more of the hormone adrenaline due to excitement and fear.

▲ The brain and nerves are made of billions of specialized cells, called nerve cells or neurons. Each has many tiny branches, dendrites, to collect nerve signals, and a longer, thicker branch, the axon or fibre, to pass on the signals.

◀ No two nerve cells touch. Instead, they transmit signals across a synapse (a tiny gap) in the form of neurotransmitters (streams of chemical particles).

190 Hormones are part of the body's inner control system. A hormone is a chemical made by a gland. It travels in the blood and affects other body parts, for example, making them work faster or release more of their product.

191 The main hormonal gland, the pituitary, is also the smallest. Just under the brain, it has close links with the nervous system. It mainly controls other hormonal glands. One is the thyroid in the neck, which affects the body's growth and how fast its chemical processes work. The pancreas controls how the body uses energy by its hormone, insulin. The adrenal glands are involved in the body's balance of water, minerals and salts, and how we react to stress and fear.

▲ Female and male bodies have much the same hormone-making glands, except for the reproductive parts — ovaries in the female (left) and testes in the male (right).

Pituitary gland

81

The brainy body

192 **Your brain is as big as your two fists side by side.** It's the place where you think, learn, work out problems, remember, feel happy and sad, wonder, worry, have ideas, sleep and dream.

▶ The two wrinkled hemispheres (halves) of the cerebrum are the largest parts of the brain.. This is where thinking happens.

193 **The brain looks like a wrinkly lump of grey-pink jelly!** On average, it weighs about 1.4 kilograms. It doesn't move, but its amazing nerve activity uses up one-fifth of all the energy needed by the body.

▼ Different areas or centres of the brain's outer layer, the cerebral cortex, deal with messages from and to certain parts of the body.

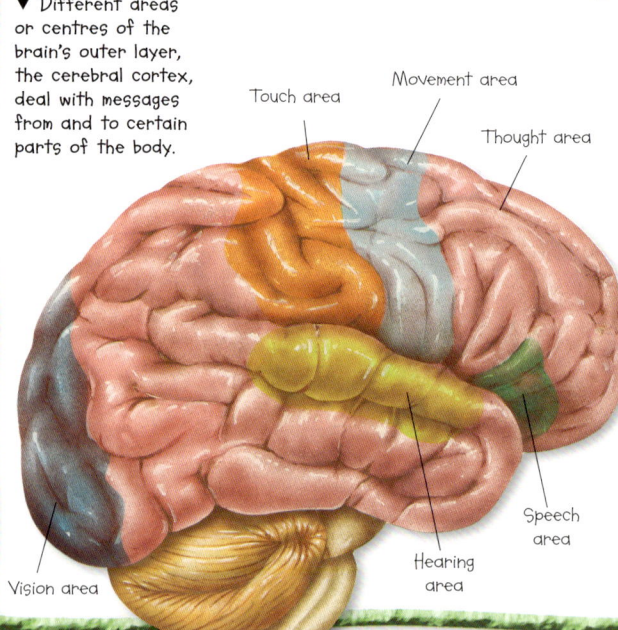

194 **The main part of the brain is its bulging, wrinkled upper part, the cerebrum.** Different areas of its surface (cerebral cortex) deal with nerve signals to and from different parts of the body. For example, messages from the eyes pass to the lower rear part of the cerebrum, called the visual centre. They are sorted here as the brain cells work out what the eyes are seeing. There are also areas for touch, hearing, taste and other body processes.

SCIENCE

195 **The cerebellum is the rounded, wrinkled part at the back of the brain.** It processes messages from the motor centre, sorting and coordinating them in great detail, to send to the body's hundreds of muscles. This is how we learn skilled, precise movements such as writing, skateboarding or playing music (or all three), almost without thinking.

196 **The brain stem is the lower part of the brain, where it joins the body's main nerve, the spinal cord.** The brain stem controls basic processes vital for life, like breathing, heartbeat, digesting food and removing wastes.

197 **The brain really does have 'brain waves'.** Every second it receives, sorts and sends millions of nerve signals. Special pads attached to the head can detect these tiny electrical pulses. They are shown on a screen or paper strip as wavy lines called an EEG, electro-encephalogram.

▲ Our brains allow us to draw from memory, expressing emotions.

I DON'T BELIEVE IT!

The brain never sleeps! EEG waves show that it is almost as busy at night as when we are awake. It still controls heartbeat, breathing and digestion. It also sifts through the day's events and stores memories.

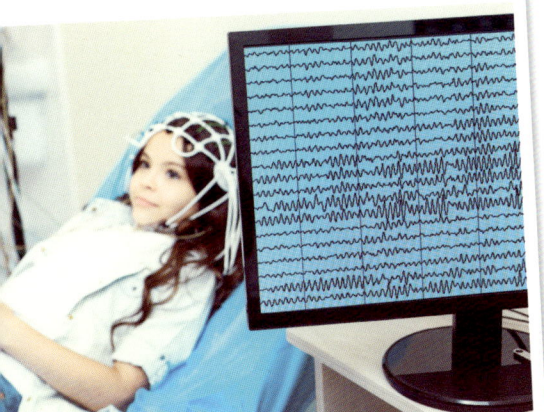

◀ The brain's 'waves' or EEG recordings change, depending on whether the person is alert and thinking hard, resting, falling asleep or deeply asleep.

DINOSAURS

198 The earliest dinosaurs stalked the Earth almost 230 million years ago. They lived in what is now Argentina, in South America. They included *Eoraptor* and *Herrerasaurus*. Both were slim and fast creatures. They could stand almost upright and run on their two rear legs. Few other animals of the time could run upright like this, on legs that were straight below their bodies. Most other animals had legs that stuck out sideways.

▲ The teeth of *Eoraptor* were suited to eating both small animal prey and soft plant foods.

The long tail balanced the head and body over the rear legs

Large head with powerful jaws contained saw-edged teeth

Each foot had three long central toes with sharp claws, and a smaller, shorter toe to each side of these

▲ *Herrerasaurus* was about 3 metres long from nose to tail. It was small, light and fast.

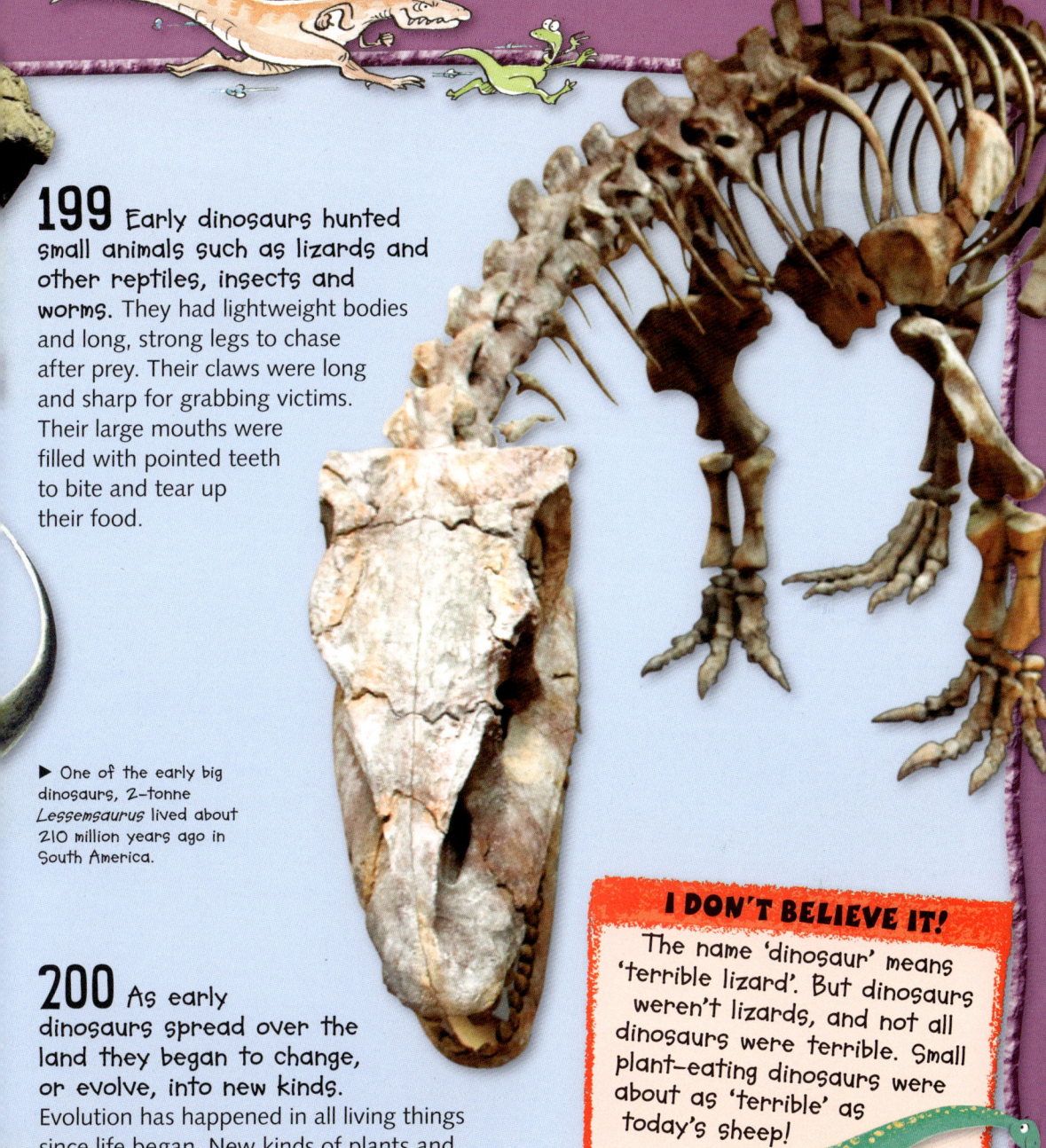

199 Early dinosaurs hunted small animals such as lizards and other reptiles, insects and worms. They had lightweight bodies and long, strong legs to chase after prey. Their claws were long and sharp for grabbing victims. Their large mouths were filled with pointed teeth to bite and tear up their food.

▶ One of the early big dinosaurs, 2-tonne *Lessemsaurus* lived about 210 million years ago in South America.

200 As early dinosaurs spread over the land they began to change, or evolve, into new kinds. Evolution has happened in all living things since life began. New kinds of plants and animals appeared, thrived for a time, and then died out. Some of the early dinosaurs evolved to be much bigger and eat plants, like 9-metre-long *Lessemsaurus*.

I DON'T BELIEVE IT!
The name 'dinosaur' means 'terrible lizard'. But dinosaurs weren't lizards, and not all dinosaurs were terrible. Small plant-eating dinosaurs were about as 'terrible' as today's sheep!

First of the giants

201 One of the first big dinosaurs well-known from fossils was *Plateosaurus*. This plant-eater lived almost 220 million years ago in what is now Europe. It grew up to 8 metres long and could rear up on its back legs and use its long neck to reach food high in trees.

Long, flexible neck for reaching food high off the ground

Sharp, jabbing claws for defence

Long, strong tail for balance

Powerful back legs for rearing up

▲ Fossils of more than 100 *Plateosaurus* have been found, so its size, shape, teeth and body details are well known compared to many other dinosaurs.

DINOSAURS

202 *Riojasaurus* was an even larger plant-eater. It lived 218 million years ago in what is now Argentina. *Riojasaurus* was 10 metres long and weighed over one tonne – as much as a large family car of today.

Small head and long, flexible neck

203 The first big plant-eating dinosaurs may have become larger, with longer necks, so that they could reach up into trees for food. Their great size would also have helped them fight enemies, since many other big meat-eating reptiles, some as long as 5 metres, were ready to make a meal of them.

◀ Like *Plateosaurus*, *Riojasaurus* was in the dinosaur group called prosauropods, with a small head, long neck and long tail.

204 These early dinosaurs lived during the first part of the Age of Dinosaurs – the Triassic Period. By its end, 200 million years ago, there were dozens of kinds of dinosaurs roaming across much of the world.

I DON'T BELIEVE IT!

Early plant-eating dinosaurs did not eat fruits or grasses – there weren't any! They hadn't appeared yet. Instead they ate plants called horsetails, ferns, cycads and conifer trees.

Super-size dinosaurs

205 **The true giants of the Age of Dinosaurs were the sauropods.** These vast dinosaurs all had a small head, long neck, barrel-shaped body, long tapering tail and four pillar-like legs. The biggest sauropods included *Brachiosaurus, Mamenchisaurus, Barosaurus, Diplodocus, Futalognkosaurus* and *Argentinosaurus*.

▼ Fossil footprints from a sauropod herd in Torotoro National Park, Bolivia.

206 **Sauropod dinosaurs probably lived in groups or herds.** We know this from their footprints, which have been preserved as fossils. Each foot left a print as large as a chair seat. Hundreds of footprints together showed many sauropods walked along with each other.

DINOSAURS

▲ *Futalognkosaurus*, a type of sauropod known as a titanosaur, was more than 30 metres long. Its name, given in 2007, means 'giant chief lizard' in the local Argentinian language.

I DON'T BELIEVE IT!

Diplodocus could swish its extremely long tail so hard and fast that it made an enormous CRACK like a whip. This living, leathery, scaly whip may have been used to scare away predators or rivals, or even rip off their skin.

207 Sauropod dinosaurs swallowed pebbles — on purpose! Their peg-like teeth could only rake in plant food, not chew it. Pebbles and stones gulped into the stomach helped to grind and crush the food. These pebbles, smooth and polished by the grinding, have been found with the fossil bones of sauropods.

209 Sauropods probably had to eat most of the time, 20 hours out of every 24. They had enormous bodies that would need great amounts of food, but only small mouths to gather it all.

▶ *Brachiosaurus* was about 25 metres long and probably weighed in the region of 30 tonnes. Its amazingly long neck allowed it to browse from the tallest trees.

208 The biggest sauropods like *Brachiosaurus* and *Futalognkosaurus* were enormous beasts. They weighed up to ten times more than elephants of today. Yet their fossil footprints showed they could run quite fast — nearly as quickly as you!

Killer claws

210 Nearly all dinosaurs had claws on their fingers and toes. These claws were shaped for different jobs in different dinosaurs. They were made from a tough substance called keratin – the same as your fingernails and toenails.

211 Hypsilophodon had strong, sturdy claws. This small 2-metre-long plant-eater probably used them to scrabble and dig in soil for seeds and roots.

212 Deinonychus had long, hooked claws on its hands. These helped it to grab victims and tear at their skin and flesh. It also had a huge hooked claw, as big as your hand, on the second toe of each foot. This could flick down like a pointed knife to slash pieces out of prey.

◀ Deinonychus, meaning 'terrible claw', probably had feathers like other raptors. It lived in North America 110 million years ago.

Long claw on each of the three fingers

Second toe had slashing 'terrible claw'

DINOSAURS

213 *Baryonyx* also had a large claw, but this was on the thumb of each hand. It may have worked as a fish-hook to snatch fish from water.

214 *Iguanodon* had claws on its feet. But these were rounded and blunt and looked more like hooves. There were also stubby claws on the fingers, while the thumb claw was longer and shaped like a spike, perhaps for stabbing enemies.

▶ Therizinosaurs, from the Cretaceous Period in Eastern Asia and Western North America, had enormous finger claws.

215 Giant sauropod dinosaurs had almost flat claws. Dinosaurs such as *Apatosaurus* looked like they had toenails on their huge feet!

▶ The long claw on *Apatosaurus*' front foot was possibly for self defence.

216 The biggest claws of any dinosaurs, and any animals, belonged to the scythe dinosaurs or therizinosaurs. Their hand claws, up to one metre long, were perhaps used to pull down and cut off leafy branches as food.

217 Therizinosaurs were big, strange-looking dinosaurs, reaching 10 metres long and 5 tonnes in weight. They lived late in the Age of Dinosaurs, and the group included *Alxasaurus*, *Nothronychus*, *Beipiaosaurus* and *Therizinosaurus*.

Deadly meat-eaters

Spinosaurus lived about 100 million years ago. It grew to 15 metres in length, and weighed as much as 10 tonnes.

About 13–14 metres in length, *Carcharodontosaurus* hunted across North Africa 95 million years ago. Its saw-edged teeth were 20 centimetres long.

Giganotosaurus was up to 13.5 metres long and had the largest skull of any meat-eating dinosaur. It lived about 97 million years ago.

218 **The biggest meat-eating dinosaurs were the largest predators ever to walk on Earth.** *Allosaurus*, which lived 150 million years ago in North America, reached almost 10 metres in length, while *Tyrannosaurus rex* from 66 million years ago was 12 metres. In South America, *Giganotosaurus* was slightly larger, while in North Africa, *Carcharodontosaurus* and *Spinosaurus* were even bigger – the largest meat-eating dinosaurs known so far.

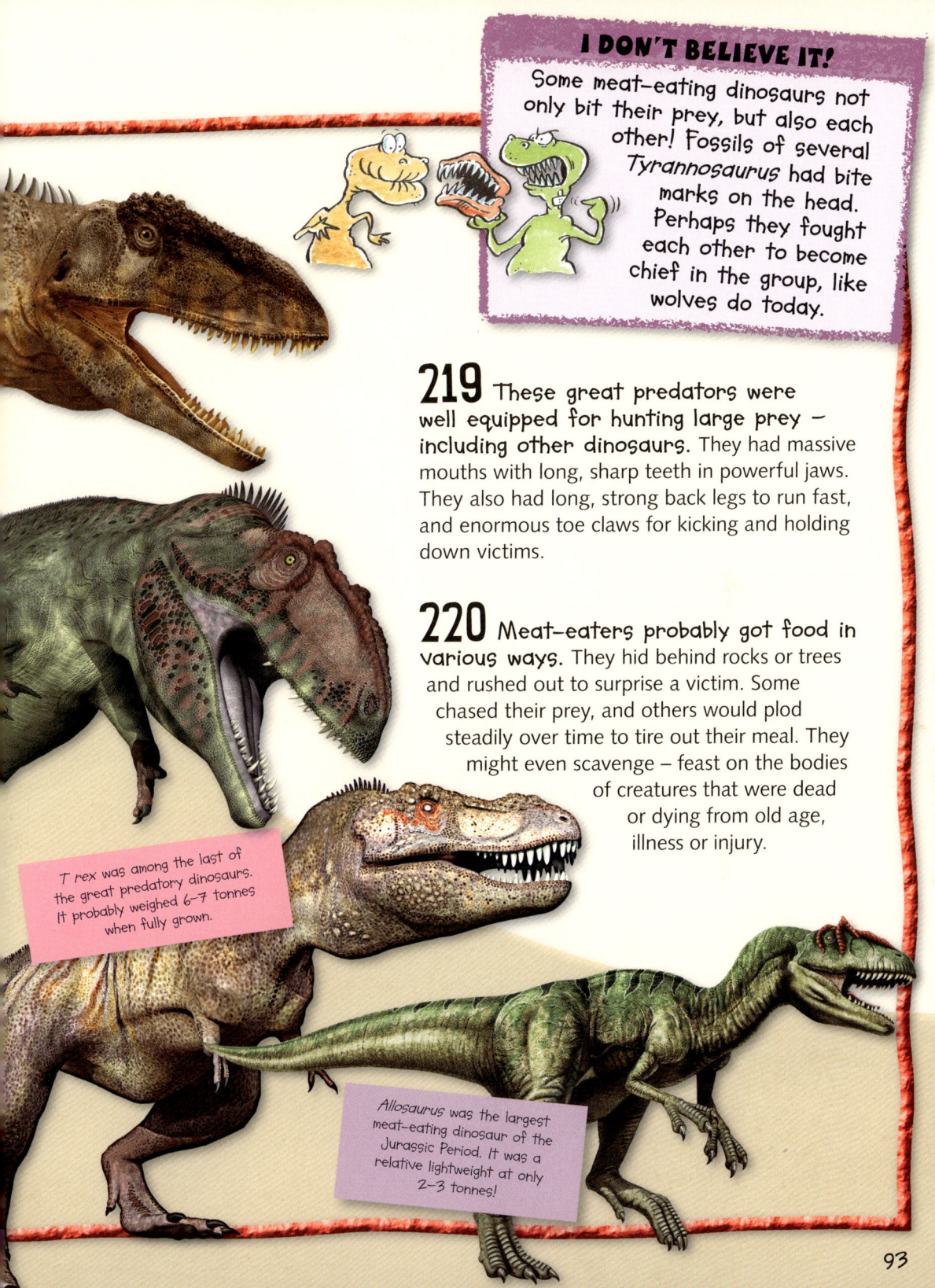

I DON'T BELIEVE IT!

Some meat-eating dinosaurs not only bit their prey, but also each other! Fossils of several *Tyrannosaurus* had bite marks on the head. Perhaps they fought each other to become chief in the group, like wolves do today.

219 These great predators were well equipped for hunting large prey — including other dinosaurs. They had massive mouths with long, sharp teeth in powerful jaws. They also had long, strong back legs to run fast, and enormous toe claws for kicking and holding down victims.

220 Meat-eaters probably got food in various ways. They hid behind rocks or trees and rushed out to surprise a victim. Some chased their prey, and others would plod steadily over time to tire out their meal. They might even scavenge — feast on the bodies of creatures that were dead or dying from old age, illness or injury.

T rex was among the last of the great predatory dinosaurs. It probably weighed 6–7 tonnes when fully grown.

Allosaurus was the largest meat-eating dinosaur of the Jurassic Period. It was a relative lightweight at only 2–3 tonnes!

Look! Listen! Sniff!

221 Like the reptiles of today, dinosaurs could see, hear and smell the world around them. We know this from fossils. The preserved fossil skulls had spaces for eyes, ears and nostrils.

222 Some dinosaurs, such as *Leaellynasaura* and *Troodon*, had big eyes. There are large, bowl-shaped hollows in their fossil skulls to allow for them. Today, animals such as mice, owls and night-time lizards can see well in the dark. Perhaps *Troodon* prowled through the forest at night, peering in the gloom for small creatures to eat.

▶ *Leaellynasaura* was a 3-metre-long plant-eater from 115 million years ago in what is now Australia.

223 There are also spaces on the sides of the head where *Troodon* had its ears. Dinosaur ears were round and flat, like the ears of other reptiles. *Troodon* could hear the tiny noises of little animals moving about in the dark.

▶ *Troodon* was about 2 metres long and lived in North America 70 million years ago.

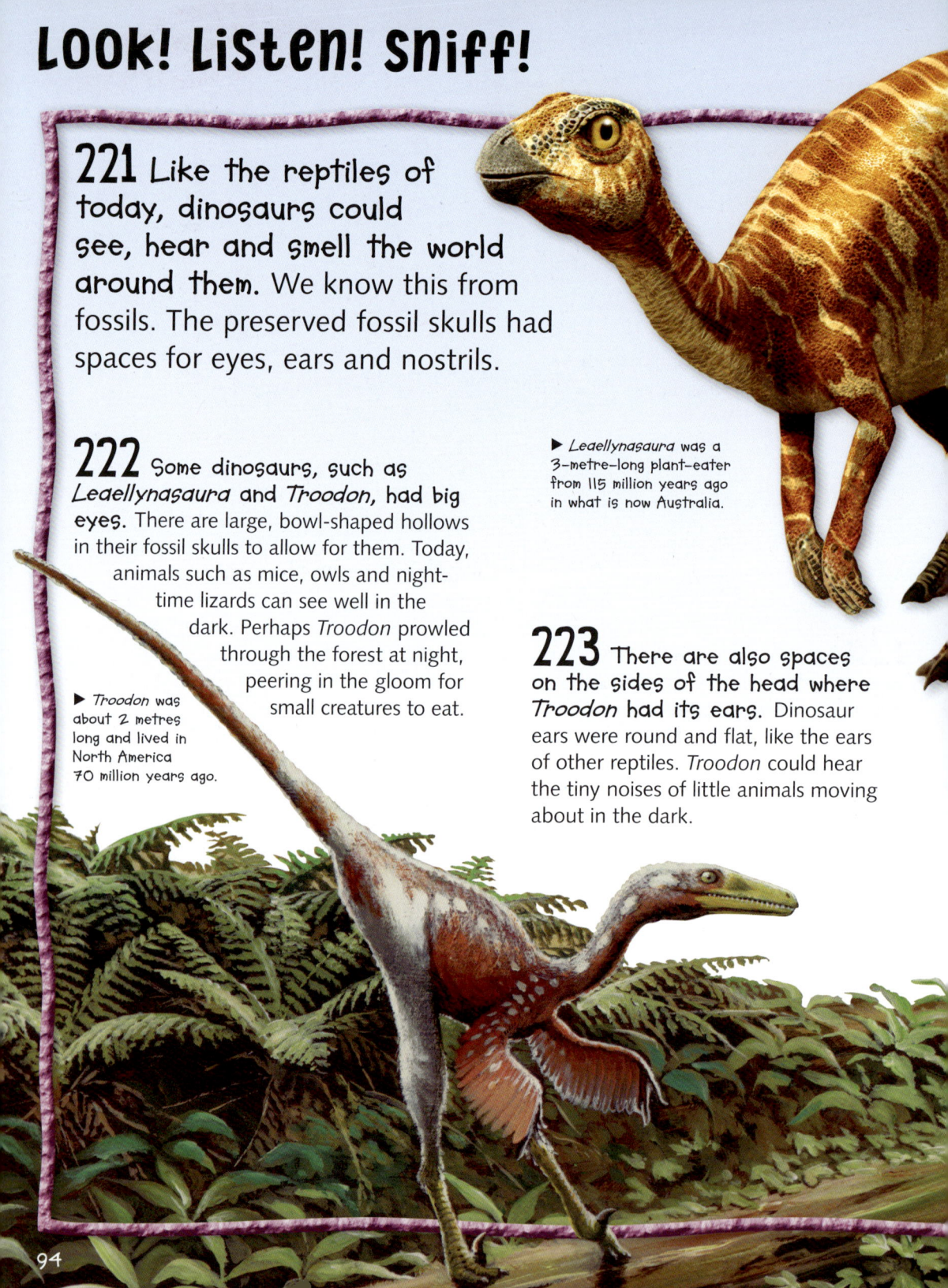

QUIZ

1. What shape were dinosaurs' ears?
2. When did *Leaellynasaura* live?
3. What did *Troodon* eat?
4. Which dinosaur had a tube-like crest on its head?

Answers:
1. Round and flat 2. 115 million years ago 3. Insects, worms, little reptiles and small shrew-like mammals 4. *Parasaurolophus*

224 The nostrils of *Troodon*, where it breathed in air and smelled scents, were two holes at the front of its snout. With its delicate sense of smell, *Troodon* could sniff out its prey of insects, worms, little reptiles such as lizards, and small shrew-like mammals.

225 Dinosaurs used their eyes, ears and noses not only to find food, but also to detect enemies — and each other. *Parasaurolophus* had a long, hollow, tube-like crest on its head. Perhaps it blew air along this to make a noise like a trumpet, as an elephant does today with its trunk.

226 Dinosaurs such as *Parasaurolophus* may have made noises to send messages to other members of their group or herd. Different messages could tell the others about finding food or warn them about enemies.

▼ *Parasaurolophus* was a 'duck-billed' dinosaur or hadrosaur. It was about 10 metres long and lived 80 million years ago in North America.

ANIMALS

227 Our planet is full of animals. They live almost everywhere, from the tops of mountains to the darkest depths of oceans. The greatest variety of animals live in places such as rainforests or coral reefs, where there is plenty of food and shelter.

▼ African animals gather round a waterhole in the dry season. The great grasslands of Africa are one of the last places where huge herds of grazing animals still survive.

228 **Animals come in all shapes and sizes.** Some, such as elephants, are giants, while others, such as fleas, are almost too small to see. There are at least five million different kinds of animals alive today, and scientists discover new kinds every day.

229 **For at least 650 million years, animals have been living on our planet.** Sponges are among the oldest known animals. They live in oceans today, but remains of sponges that lived 650 million years ago have been found preserved in Australia.

What is an animal?

230 Animals are living things that need to eat food, such as plants or other animals. This gives them the energy they need to survive. Animals use their senses to detect food and react to their surroundings.

▶ Animals can be divided into groups according to their features. Each group has certain characteristics in common.

231 An animal's body is usually made of many cells, which are grouped into tissues. Tissues may be joined together to form organs, such as the brain, heart or lungs.

Lungs for breathing

Kidneys to process waste

Brain (inside skull) to control the body

Heart to pump blood around the body

Intestines to digest food

Animal families

Invertebrates are usually small creatures, such as crabs and insects. Some have a hard shell, others are soft.

Fish live in the waters of oceans, rivers and lakes. They breathe in oxygen from the water through flaps called gills.

Amphibians, such as frogs, live partly in water and partly on land. Most lay eggs in water.

Reptiles, such as snakes and lizards, usually live on land in warm places. Most baby reptiles hatch out of eggs.

Birds have wings instead of arms, and most can fly. All birds lay eggs that have a hard shell.

Mammals, such as bears, dolphins and humans, are covered in fur or hair. They breathe air, even if they live in water.

232 Well over 90 percent of all animals are invertebrates. These animals do not have an internal backbone to support their bodies. They rely on the support of their body fluids or a hard outer casing, called an exoskeleton.

◀ The organs inside a chimpanzee are very similar to those inside a human being.

ANIMALS

233 **Animals with a backbone are called vertebrates.** Their backbone forms part of an internal skeleton, which is usually made of bone. However, sharks and rays have a skeleton made of rubbery cartilage. A skeleton supports the body, helps it to move and protects the internal organs.

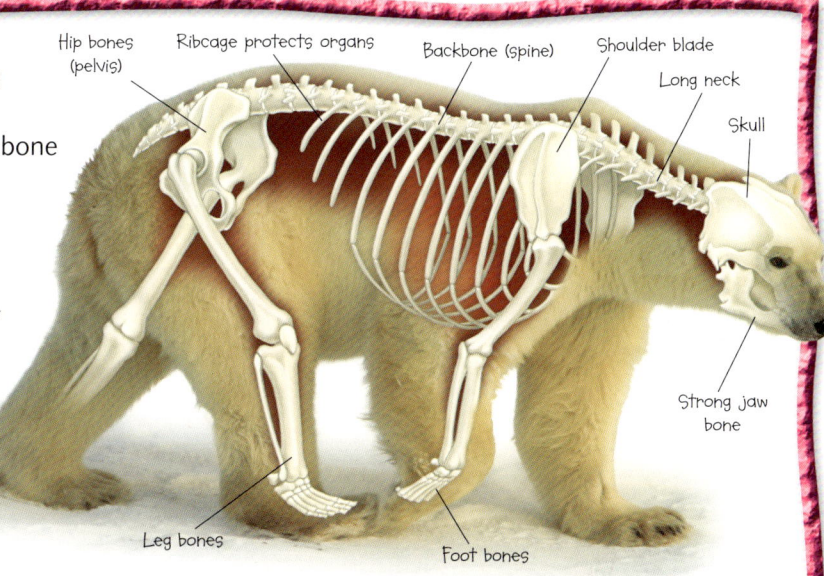

▲ A polar bear has a short, strong backbone and powerful leg and hip bones. Its skull is long and slim to help it swim.

234 **Vertebrates have different coverings on the outsides of their bodies.** Fish and reptiles have scales made from hard skin or bone. Frogs usually have smooth skin. Birds are the only animals with feathers, and mammals are the only animals with fur or hair.

▶ Foals will feed from their mothers for several months, or up to one year in the wild.

235 **Humans are mammals.** Mammals are the most intelligent of all animals. Female mammals feed their young on milk, which they produce themselves. There are about 5500 different kinds of mammals and up to one-quarter of them are bats!

99

Super senses

236 Animals sense the world around them through seeing, hearing, smelling, touching and tasting. An animal's senses also supply information about its own body, such as whether it is too hot or too cold.

Sight

▶ A fly's huge compound eyes are good at picking up movement over a wide area. The fly's brain puts together the images from all the eye units to create a complete picture.

Hearing

Ears move backwards and forwards to detect danger

237 Many animals have eyes to detect light. Insects have compound eyes made up of hundreds of tiny eyes with one or more lenses. Animals with bigger eyes may have a slit in the middle of the eye called a pupil, which controls the amount of light entering the eye.

238 Mammals are the only animals with ear flaps that funnel sounds into the ear. The sounds hit an eardrum, which vibrates. Tiny bones pass on the vibrations to a fluid-filled chamber in the inner ear. Receptors in the inner ear send signals to the mammal's brain, which 'hears' the sound.

◀ A rabbit's big ears can be turned in different directions to locate the source of a sound, or even listen to two sounds at the same time.

ANIMALS

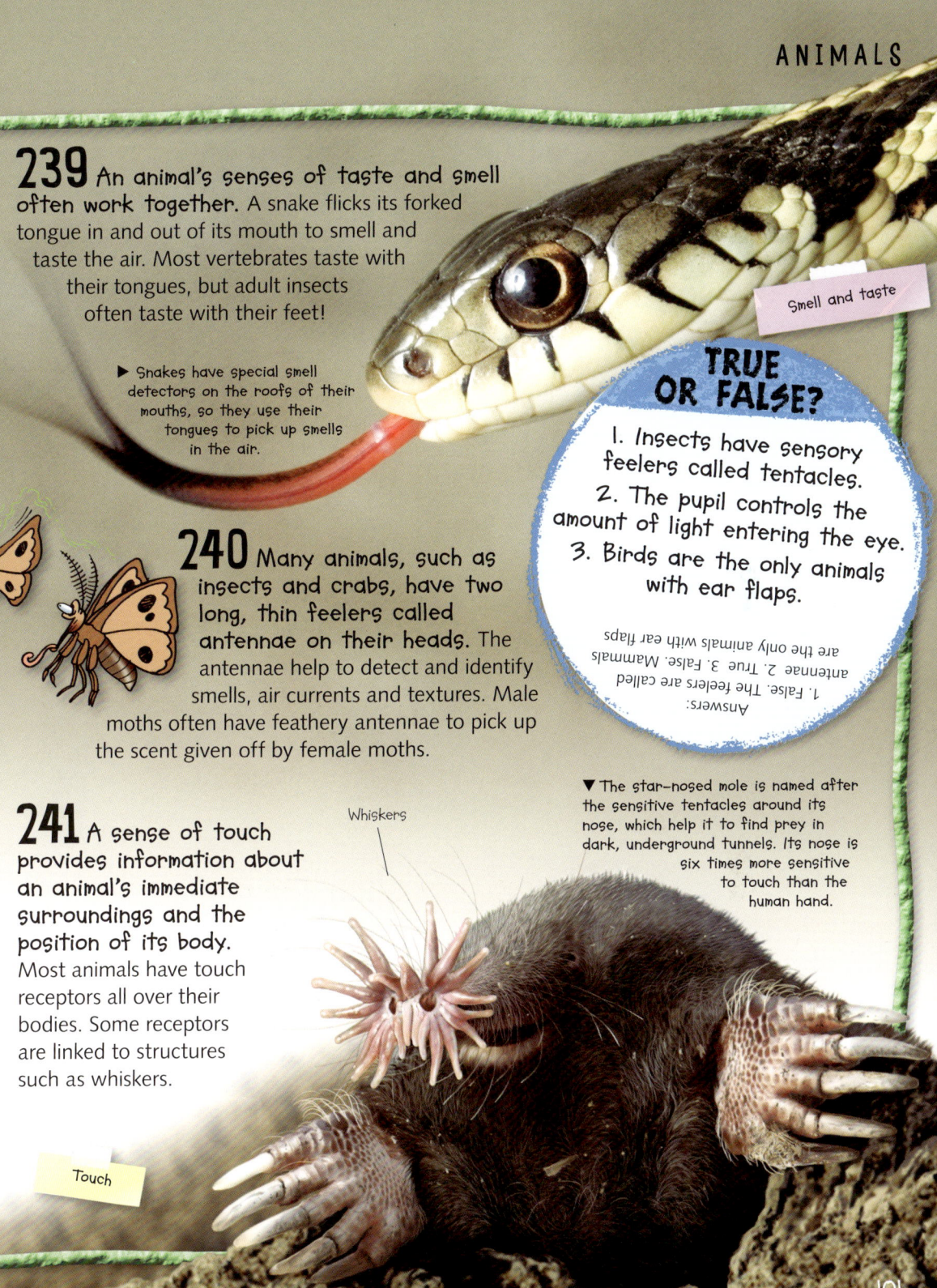

239 **An animal's senses of taste and smell often work together.** A snake flicks its forked tongue in and out of its mouth to smell and taste the air. Most vertebrates taste with their tongues, but adult insects often taste with their feet!

▶ Snakes have special smell detectors on the roofs of their mouths, so they use their tongues to pick up smells in the air.

Smell and taste

TRUE OR FALSE?

1. Insects have sensory feelers called tentacles.
2. The pupil controls the amount of light entering the eye.
3. Birds are the only animals with ear flaps.

Answers:
1. False. The feelers are called antennae 2. True 3. False. Mammals are the only animals with ear flaps

240 **Many animals, such as insects and crabs, have two long, thin feelers called antennae on their heads.** The antennae help to detect and identify smells, air currents and textures. Male moths often have feathery antennae to pick up the scent given off by female moths.

Whiskers

241 **A sense of touch provides information about an animal's immediate surroundings and the position of its body.** Most animals have touch receptors all over their bodies. Some receptors are linked to structures such as whiskers.

▼ The star-nosed mole is named after the sensitive tentacles around its nose, which help it to find prey in dark, underground tunnels. Its nose is six times more sensitive to touch than the human hand.

Touch

101

Predators and prey

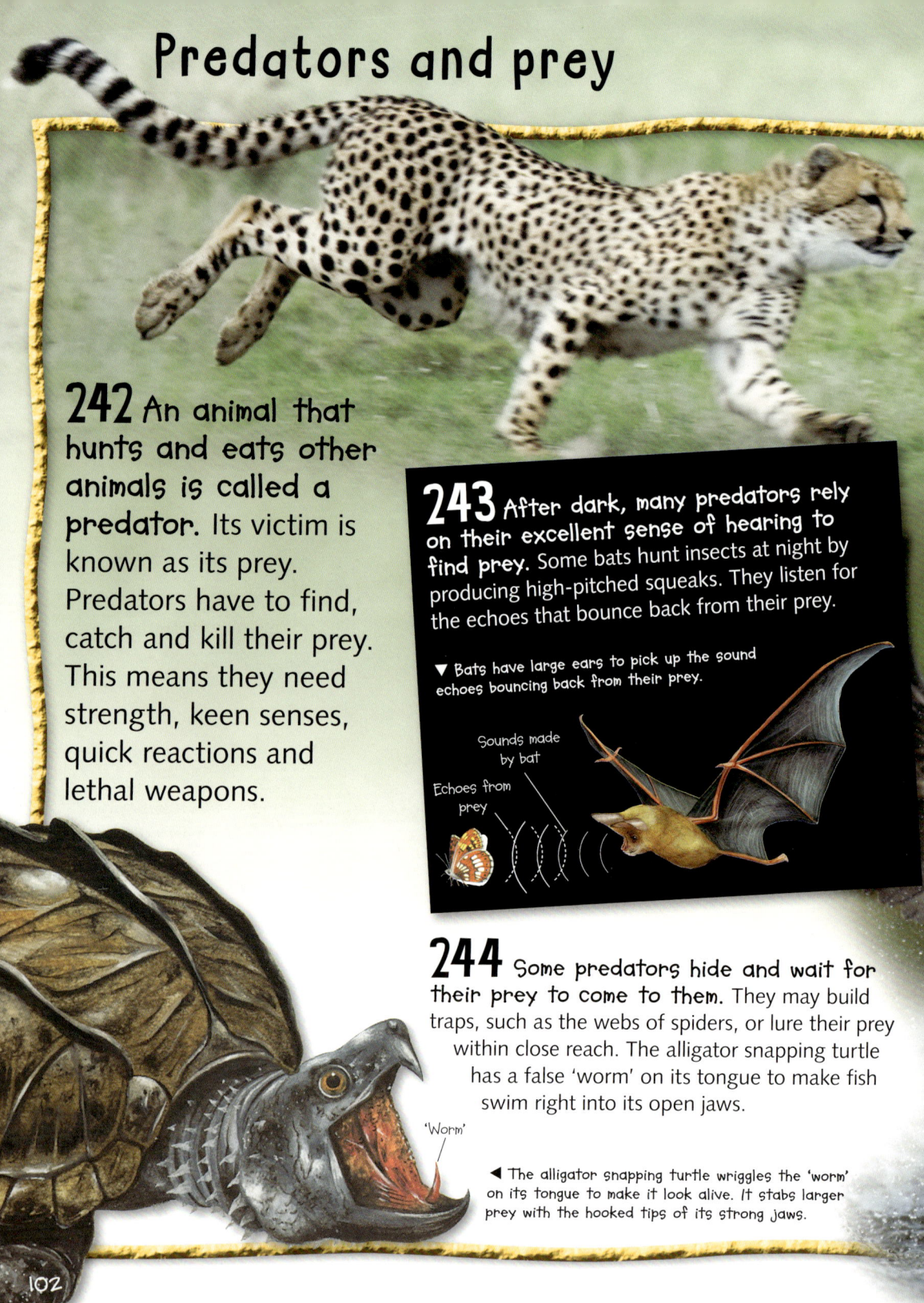

242 **An animal that hunts and eats other animals is called a predator.** Its victim is known as its prey. Predators have to find, catch and kill their prey. This means they need strength, keen senses, quick reactions and lethal weapons.

243 **After dark, many predators rely on their excellent sense of hearing to find prey.** Some bats hunt insects at night by producing high-pitched squeaks. They listen for the echoes that bounce back from their prey.

▼ Bats have large ears to pick up the sound echoes bouncing back from their prey.

Sounds made by bat
Echoes from prey

244 **Some predators hide and wait for their prey to come to them.** They may build traps, such as the webs of spiders, or lure their prey within close reach. The alligator snapping turtle has a false 'worm' on its tongue to make fish swim right into its open jaws.

'Worm'

◀ The alligator snapping turtle wriggles the 'worm' on its tongue to make it look alive. It stabs larger prey with the hooked tips of its strong jaws.

ANIMALS

I DON'T BELIEVE IT!
A great white shark has about 300 razor-sharp teeth in its mouth. Its jaws open wide enough to swallow a whole seal in one big gulp!

◄► A cheetah can only run at top speed for a few hundred metres before it gets too hot and exhausted, and has to stop. If this warthog keeps running, it might get away.

245 Active predators need a set of weapons for attacking and killing their prey without being injured themselves. These weapons range from pointed teeth and powerful jaws, to curved claws, sharp bills and poisonous stings or fangs.

◄ Ospreys use their strong, needle-sharp claws, called talons, to snatch fish from the water. Spines under their toes help them to hold their slippery prey.

246 Many spiders are agile, fast-moving hunters that stalk their prey. Jumping spiders prowl around, using their eight eyes to spot a meal. They pounce on their prey and kill it with a bite from their poisonous fangs. Some predators save energy by sneaking up on their prey, then attacking suddenly at the last minute. Many are well camouflaged so they can creep close to their prey.

► Chameleons creep very slowly along branches, but they shoot out their long, sticky tongues at lightning speed to catch insects.

Mammals

Placental mammals

247 **There are nearly 5500 different types of mammal.** Most have babies that grow inside the mother's body. While the baby grows, a special organ called a placenta supplies it with food and oxygen from the mother's body. These mammals are called placental mammals.

Placenta   Birth canal

▲ A baby elephant in the womb receives nourishment through the placenta.

248 **Not all mammals' young develop inside the mother's body.** Two smaller groups of mammals do things differently. Monotremes, such as platypuses and echidnas (spiny anteaters), lay eggs. The platypus lays her eggs in a burrow, but the echidna keeps her single egg in a special pouch in her belly until it is ready to hatch.

▶ The echidna keeps her egg in a pouch until it hatches after about ten days.

Monotremes

249 **Mammal mothers feed their babies on milk from their own bodies.** The baby sucks this milk from teats on special mammary glands, also called udders or breasts, on the mother's body. The milk contains all the food the young animal needs to help it grow.

ANIMALS

250 **Marsupials give birth to tiny young that finish developing in a pouch.** A baby kangaroo is only 2 centimetres long when it is born. Tiny, blind and hairless, it makes its own way to the safety of its mother's pouch. Once there, it latches onto a teat in the pouch and begins to feed.

A joey starts life as a tiny undeveloped baby

Marsupials

▲ A baby kangaroo is called a joey. It stays in the pouch for about six months while it grows.

▼ This reindeer uses its eyes, its ears and especially its nose to sense the world.

251 **Most mammals have good senses of sight, smell and hearing.** Their senses help them watch out for enemies, find food and keep in touch with each other. For many mammals, smell is their most important sense. Plant-eaters such as rabbits and deer sniff the air to pick up scents of danger, especially those of predators.

I DON'T BELIEVE IT!
Lemmings are very fast breeders. Females can become pregnant at only 14 days old, and they can produce litters of as many as 12 young every month.

The bird world

252 There are over 9000 different types, or species, of bird. These have been organized by scientists into 29 groups called orders, which contain many different species. The largest of these is the Passeriformes order.

▼ This chaffinch is in the Passeriformes order. More than half of all bird species belong to this order.

Passeriformes order: Includes robins, sparrows and wrens

- Common swift — Apodiformes order: Swifts and hummingbirds
- Keel-billed toucan — Piciformes order: Toucans and woodpeckers
- Blue-and-yellow macaw — Psittaciformes order: Parrots, cockatoos and lorikeets
- Pied avocet — Charadriiformes order: Waders, gulls and auks

▲ The shape of a bird's beak can be used to decide which order a bird belongs to. These pictures show examples from the largest orders.

253 All birds have wings. These are the bird's front limbs and they come in many different shapes. Birds that soar in the sky for hours, such as eagles, have long, broad wings. Small, fast-flying birds such as swifts have slim, pointed wings.

▶ Feathers have different shapes, sizes and textures, suited to the jobs they do.

- Tail feather
- Flight feather
- Contour (body) feather
- Down feather

254 Birds are the only creatures that have feathers. They are made of keratin — the same material as our hair and nails. Feathers keep a bird warm, and its wing and tail feathers help it to fly. Some birds have colourful feathers to help attract mates or blend in with their surroundings — camouflage.

ANIMALS

255 All birds have a beak, or bill, for eating. The beak is made of bone and is covered with a hard material called horn. Birds have different kinds of beak for different types of food. Insect-eating birds tend to have thin, sharp beaks for picking up their tiny prey. The parrot's strong beak is ideal for cracking nuts. Hunting birds, such as goshawks, have powerful hooked beaks for tearing flesh.

QUIZ

1. How many types of bird are there?
2. What is the largest order of birds called?
3. What are feathers made of?
4. What shape is a hunting bird's beak?

Answers:
1. Over 9000 2. The Passeriformes order 3. Keratin 4. Hooked

256 Birds lay eggs. It would be impossible for birds to carry their developing young inside their bodies like mammals do – they would be too heavy to fly.

▼ The egg protects the growing chick and provides it with food. While the young develop, the parent birds, such as this common eider, keep the eggs safe and warm. This is called incubation.

107

Scales and slime

Reptile family

Over half of all reptiles are lizards — there are nearly 5000 species.

Amphisbaenians, or worm lizards, are burrowing reptiles that live underground.

Tuataras are rare, ancient and unusual reptiles from New Zealand.

Snakes are the second largest group of reptiles.

Crocodiles, alligators, gharials and caimans are predators with sharp teeth.

Turtles and tortoises have hard shells that protect them from predators.

257 **Reptiles and amphibians are cold-blooded animals.** There are four kinds of reptiles — snakes, lizards and amphisbaenians, the crocodile family, tortoises and turtles, and the tuataras. Amphibians are split into frogs and toads, newts and salamanders, and caecilians.

258 **Reptiles do a lot of sunbathing!** Sitting in the sun is called basking — reptiles bask to warm themselves with the Sun's heat so they can move. When it gets cold, at night or during a cold season, reptiles might hibernate, which is a type of deep sleep.

▶ Blue-collared lizards may bask for many hours at a time.

259 **Most reptiles have dry, scaly, waterproof skin.** This stops their bodies from drying out. The scales are made of keratin and may form thick, tough plates. Human nails are made of the same material.

Amphibian family

Newts have slender bodies and long tails.

Frogs have smooth skin and long legs for jumping.

Toads often have warty skin and crawl or walk.

Salamanders have tails and they usually have bright markings.

Caecilians are burrowing animals without legs.

ANIMALS

▼ Green-skinned frogs can hide among leaves and pondweed.

260 **Amphibians have skin that is moist, smooth and soft.** Oxygen can pass easily through their skin, which is important because most adult amphibians breathe through their skin as well as with their lungs. Reptiles breathe only with their lungs.

261 **Amphibians' skin is kept moist by special glands just under the surface.** These glands produce a sticky substance called mucus. Many amphibians also keep their skin moist by making sure that they are never far away from water.

262 **Some amphibians have no lungs.** Humans breathe with their lungs to get oxygen from the air and breathe out carbon dioxide. Most amphibians breathe through their skin and lungs, but lungless salamanders breathe only through their skin and the lining of the mouth.

QUIZ
1. Why do reptiles bask?
2. How do most amphibians breathe?
3. How do reptiles breathe?

Answers:
1. To warm themselves with the Sun's heat so they can move 2. Through their skin and with their lungs 3. With their lungs

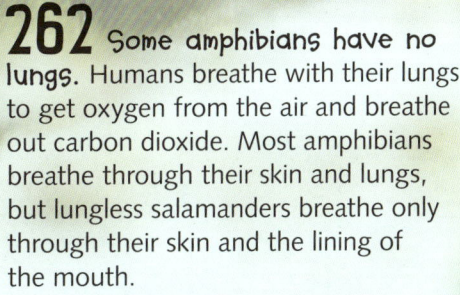

Shark!

263 Nearly all sharks have slim, streamlined bodies. This makes them fast swimmers – they slip through the water easily and travel at speed. One of the fastest sharks is the shortfin mako. It swims at more than 55 kilometres an hour – much faster than a champion human sprinter can run.

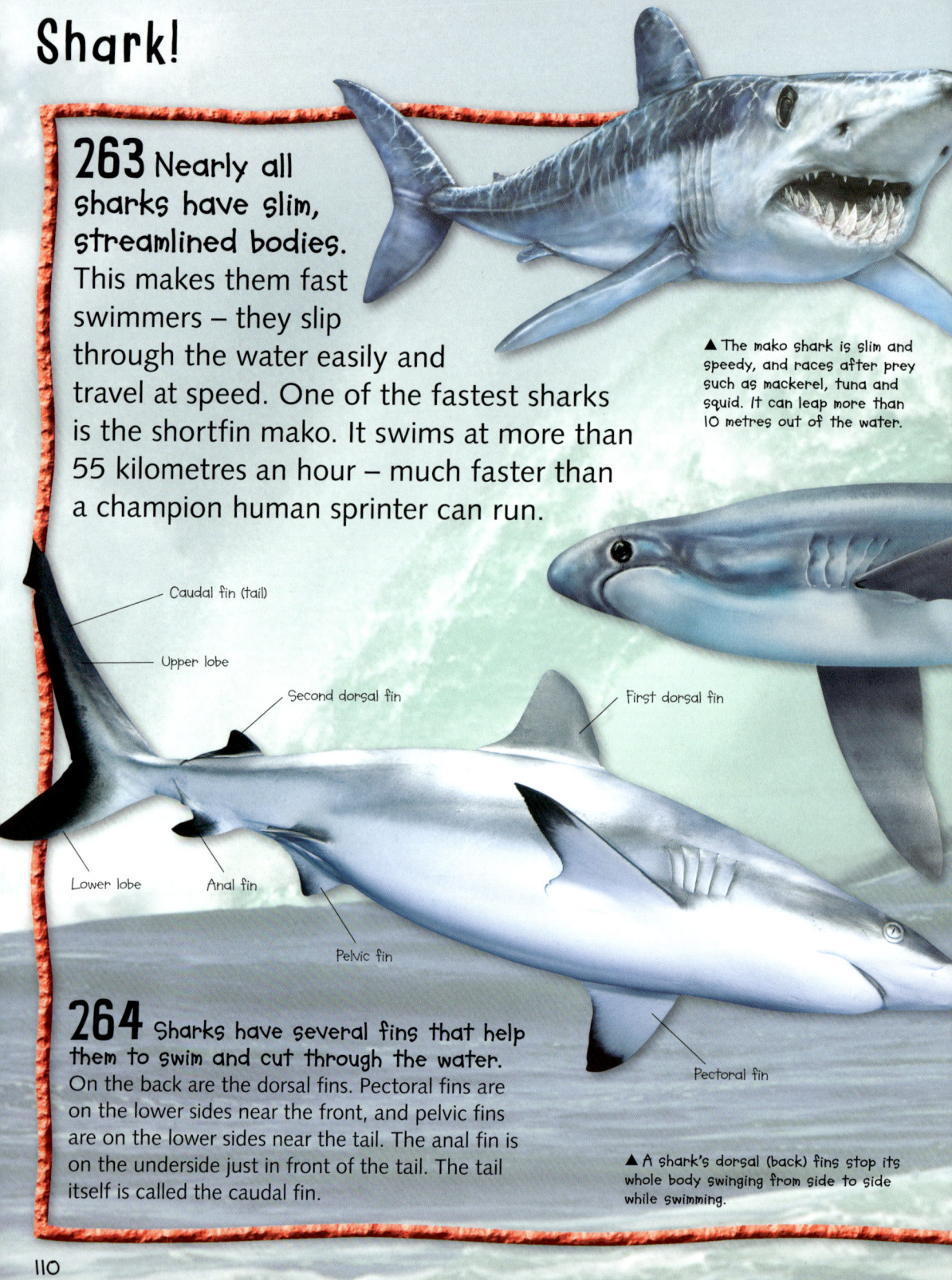

▲ The mako shark is slim and speedy, and races after prey such as mackerel, tuna and squid. It can leap more than 10 metres out of the water.

Caudal fin (tail)
Upper lobe
Second dorsal fin
First dorsal fin
Lower lobe
Anal fin
Pelvic fin
Pectoral fin

264 Sharks have several fins that help them to swim and cut through the water. On the back are the dorsal fins. Pectoral fins are on the lower sides near the front, and pelvic fins are on the lower sides near the tail. The anal fin is on the underside just in front of the tail. The tail itself is called the caudal fin.

▲ A shark's dorsal (back) fins stop its whole body swinging from side to side while swimming.

265 **Some sharks have tails longer than their bodies.** The common thresher shark is 6 metres long – and half of this is its tail. The thresher uses it to attack smaller fish, so it can eat them.

▼ The thresher shark thrashes its tail from side to side to stun small fish before swallowing them.

266 **Shark tails have other uses, too.** Some sharks smack the water's surface with their tails to frighten their prey. Others swish away sand or mud on the seabed to reveal any hidden creatures.

QUIZ

1. How many gills do most sharks have – 5, 10 or 12?
2. Where are a shark's dorsal fins – on its back or its underside?
3. What do gills take in from water?

Answers:
1. 10 (5 pairs) 2. On its back 3. Oxygen

BREATHING UNDERWATER

1. Most sharks have five pairs of gills
2. Fine blood vessels allow oxygen to pass from the water to the blood
3. Heart pumps blood around the body

▶ A shark's gill chambers are in its neck region. Most have five gill slits on either side.

267 **Like other fish, sharks breathe underwater using their gills.** These are under the slits on either side of the head, and are filled with blood. Water flows in through the shark's mouth, over the gills and out through the slits. The gills take in oxygen from the water because sharks need oxygen to survive.

268 **Most sharks swim all of the time so that water flows over their gills and they can breathe.** However some can lie still and make the water flow over their gills by 'pumping' the muscles of their mouth and neck.

Insects everywhere

269 **The housefly is one of the most common, widespread and annoying insects.** There are many other members of the fly group, such as bluebottles, horseflies, craneflies and fruitflies. They all have two wings. Most other kinds of insects have four wings.

▼ Insects, such as this horsefly, do not have a bony skeleton like we do. Their bodies are covered by horny plates, called an exoskeleton.

Wings are clear or with a yellowish tinge

Dark colouring

Large, stocky body, 1–2.5 centimetres long

Short antennae

Very large eyes, which are widely separated in females, but joined in males

270 **The ladybird is a noticeable insect with its bright red or yellow body, and black spots.** It is a member of the beetle group – the biggest insect group of all. There are more than half a million kinds, from massive Goliath beetles to tiny flea beetles.

▶ Bright colours warn other animals that ladybirds taste horrible.

271 **The cabbage white butterfly is not usually welcome in the garden.** Its young, known as caterpillars, eat the leaves of plants. There are around 17,500 kinds of butterflies, and even more kinds of moths – about 160,000!

▼ When the earwig is threatened, it raises its tail to try to make itself look bigger.

272 **The earwig is a familiar insect outside – and sometimes inside.** Despite their name, earwigs do not crawl into ears or hide in wigs, but they do like dark, damp corners. Earwigs form one of the smaller insect groups, with fewer than 2000 different kinds.

ANIMALS

273 **Ants are fine in the garden or wood, but are pests in the house.** Ants, bees and wasps make up a large insect group with some 130,000 different kinds. Most can sting, although many are too small to hurt people. However, some types, such as bulldog ants, have a painful bite.

▶ Ants use their antennae and sense of touch as a means of communication. These ants are forming a 'living bridge' so their fellow workers can cross a gap to reach food.

274 **The scorpionfly has a nasty-looking sting on a long curved tail.** It flies or crawls around bushes and weeds during summer. Only the male scorpionfly has the red tail. It looks like the sting of a scorpion, but is harmless.

I DON'T BELIEVE IT!
Green tiger beetles are about 12–15 millimetres long but can run at about 60–70 centimetres per second. That is like a human sprinter running 100 metres in one second!

113

Awesome arachnids

275 Not all creepy-crawlies are insects. Spiders, scorpions, mites and ticks all belong to a different group called arachnids. Arachnids have eight legs – all insects have six.

276 All spiders can make thin, fine threads called silk. These come out of spinnerets at the rear of the spider. About half of the 40,000 kinds of spiders make webs to catch prey. Some spiders make silk bags, called cocoons, to lay their eggs in or create protective 'nursery tents' for their young.

Front legs wrap silk around prey

▲ This argiope spider has caught a grasshopper in its web. It wraps its prey in silk to stop it moving.

▶ The hardest part of building a web is getting the first thread in place. The spider needs a gust of wind to carry the thread across, so it sticks to a good spot.

❶ The first thread is horizontal

❷ The second thread makes a Y-shape

❸ More strands, called radials, are added

❹ A temporary spiral is put in place

❺ The final spiral is built more carefully

ANIMALS

▼ This scorpion is attacking a grasshopper.

Stinger on last tail part

Pedipalp claws grab prey

277 Scorpions live in warm parts of the world. The scorpion has large, crab-like pincers called pedipalps to grab its prey, and powerful jaws like scissors to chop it up. It also has a venomous sting at the tip of its tail, which it can use this to paralyze or kill a victim.

278 The sun spider or solifuge is another very fierce, spider-like hunter. It has no venom, but it does have a pair of very large jaws. Most kinds live in deserts and are known as camel spiders.

I DON'T BELIEVE IT!
Some mites are so small that a handful of soil may contain half a million of them.

ANCIENT HISTORY

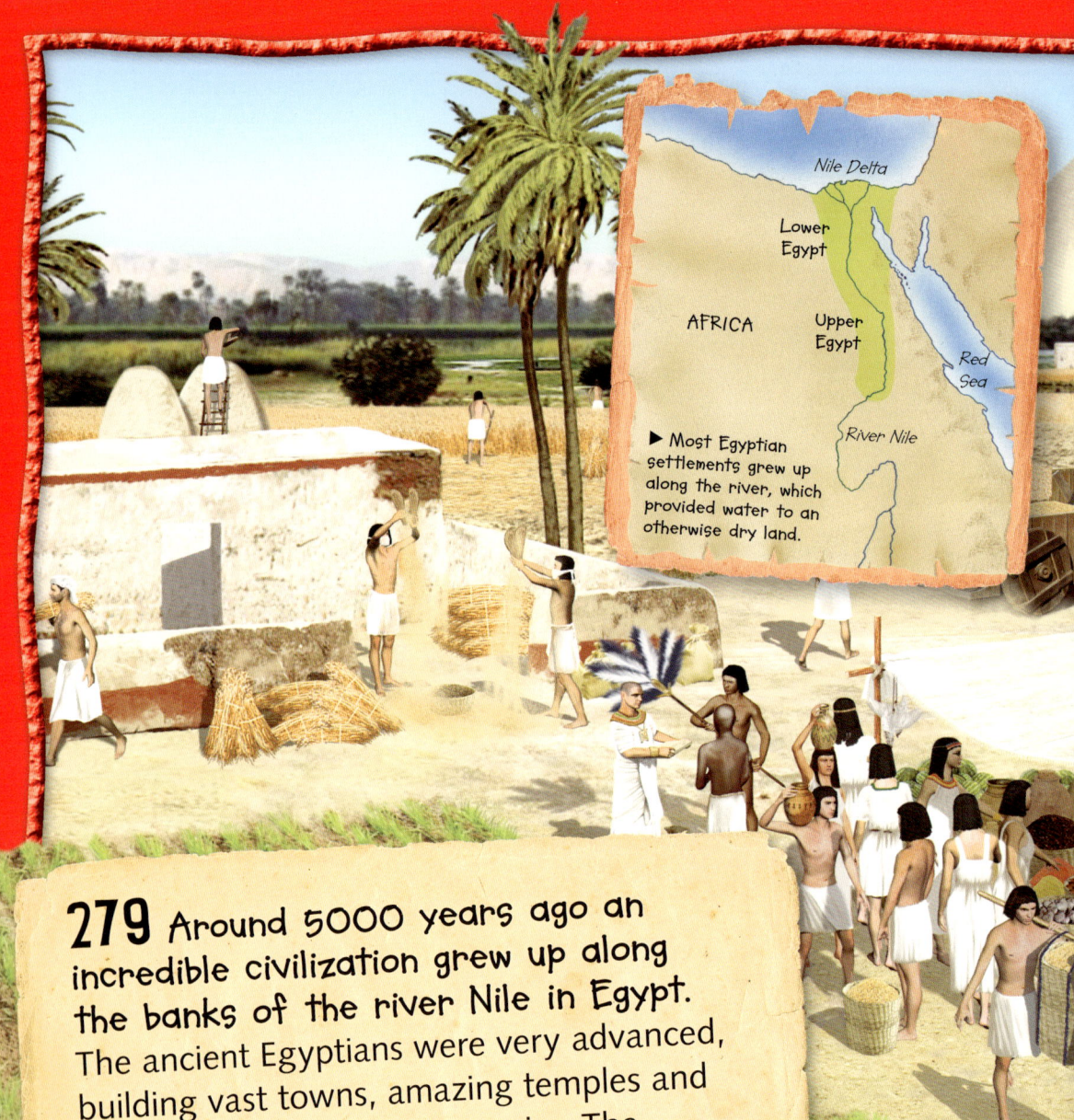

▶ Most Egyptian settlements grew up along the river, which provided water to an otherwise dry land.

279 Around 5000 years ago an incredible civilization grew up along the banks of the river Nile in Egypt. The ancient Egyptians were very advanced, building vast towns, amazing temples and tombs and an impressive empire. The civilization lasted for over 3000 years, from around 3100–30 BC, when the Romans conquered Egypt.

▼ The Nile supported many activities such as trade and farming. It was also an important transportation route, with people and goods travelling by boat.

280 The Nile allowed the ancient Egyptians to flourish. It was their main form of transport and provided water for drinking and watering crops. Every year its floods left a strip of rich, dark soil on both sides of the river where farmers grew crops. The Egyptians called their country *Kemet*, which means 'black land', after this dark soil. The Nile was also an important trade route.

Powerful pharaohs

281 The rulers of ancient Egypt were called pharaohs. The word 'pharaoh' means great house. The pharaoh was the most important and powerful person in the country. Many people believed he was a god. Officials called viziers helped the pharaoh to govern Egypt.

I DON'T BELIEVE IT!
On special occasions, women wore hair cones made of animal fat scented with spices and herbs. The fat melted, trickling down their heads, making their hair greasy but sweet-smelling!

▼ These people are paying tribute to the pharaoh. They have come from nearby countries to pay him respect and offer him gifts.

The pharaoh is holding the symbols of his rule — the hook (right) and flail (left)

ANCIENT HISTORY

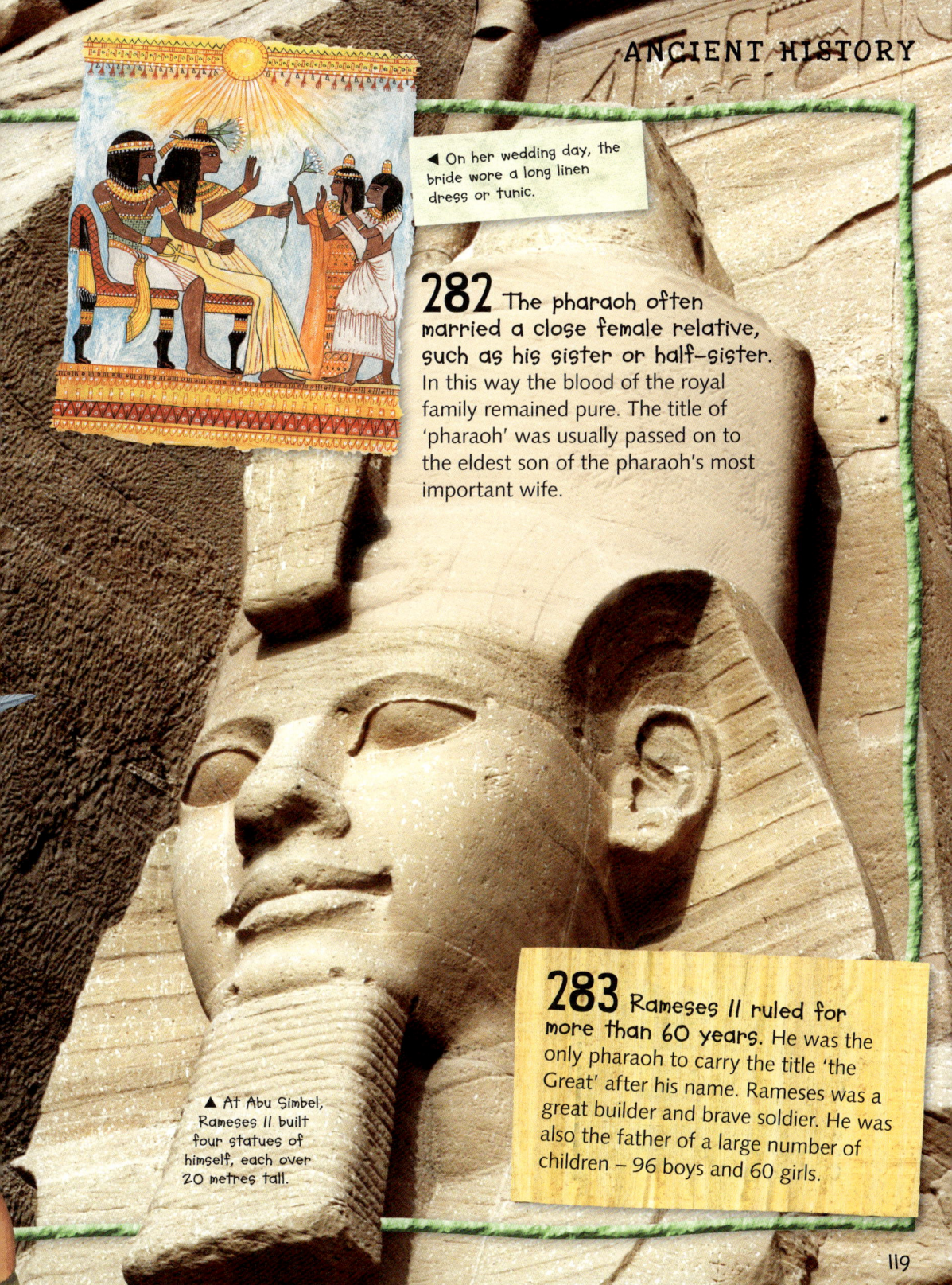

◀ On her wedding day, the bride wore a long linen dress or tunic.

282 The pharaoh often married a close female relative, such as his sister or half-sister. In this way the blood of the royal family remained pure. The title of 'pharaoh' was usually passed on to the eldest son of the pharaoh's most important wife.

▲ At Abu Simbel, Rameses II built four statues of himself, each over 20 metres tall.

283 Rameses II ruled for more than 60 years. He was the only pharaoh to carry the title 'the Great' after his name. Rameses was a great builder and brave soldier. He was also the father of a large number of children – 96 boys and 60 girls.

Magnificent monuments

284 The pyramids at Giza are more than 4500 years old. They were built for three kings, Khufu, Khafre and Menkaure. The biggest, the Great Pyramid, took more than 20 years to build. Thousands of workers were needed to complete the job.

Pyramid of Menkaure

Pyramid of Khafre

▶ The Great Pyramid is built from over two million blocks of limestone. It stands about 140 metres high.

Mastabas (tombs for the nobility)

King's chamber

Queen's chamber

Underground chamber

Great Pyramid of Khufu

Mortuary temple

Queens' pyramids

QUIZ

1. For which king was the Great Pyramid built?
2. In the Great Pyramid, which corridor lead to the king's chamber?
3. Where was the first step pyramid built?

Answers:
1. King Khufu 2. The Grand Gallery 3. Saqqara

285 The Great Pyramid, the biggest of the three pyramids, was built as a burial place for King Khufu. He ordered three smaller pyramids to be built beside it – for his three main wives. The boat that probably carried Khufu's body to his tomb was buried in a pit alongside the pyramid.

ANCIENT HISTORY

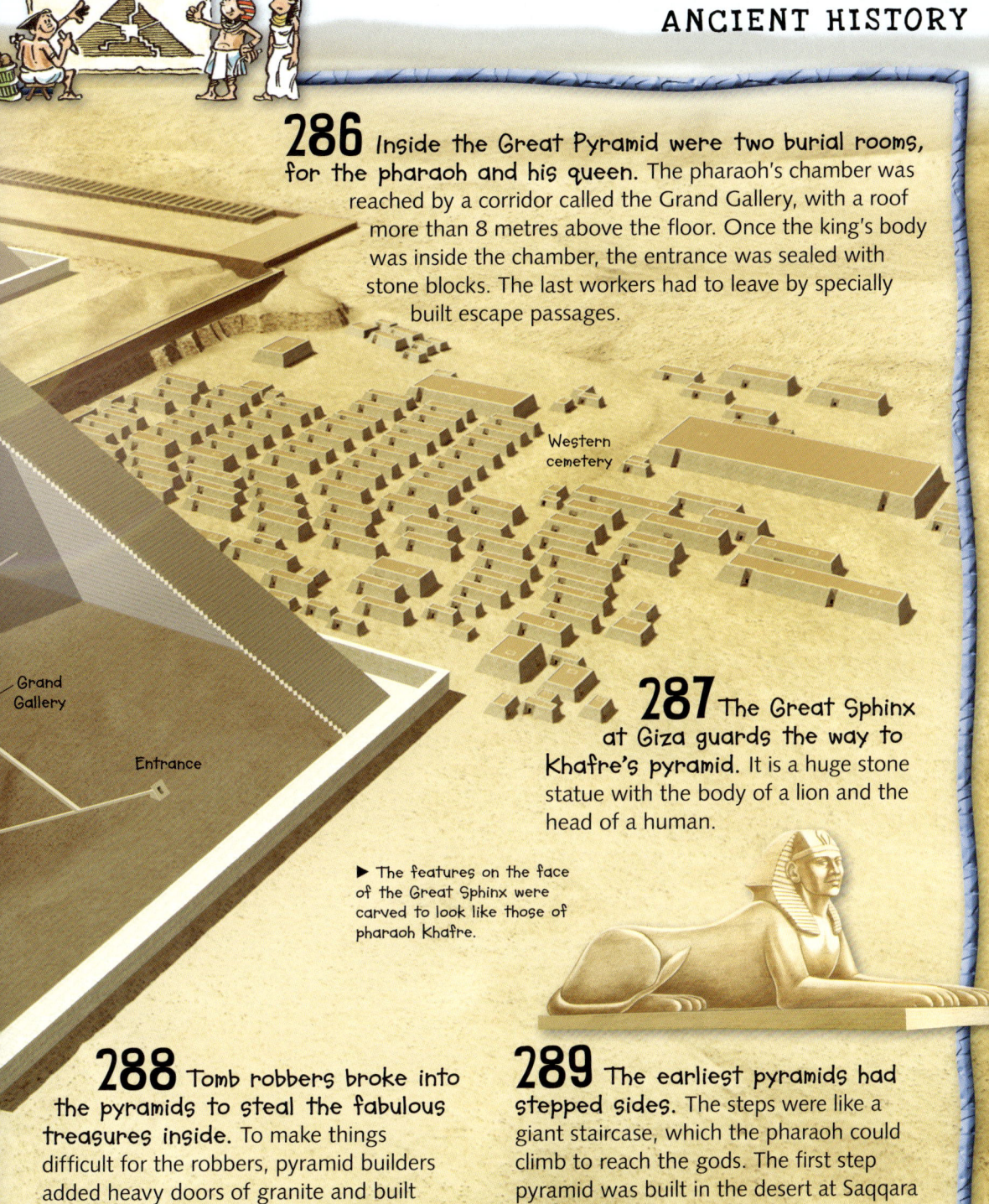

286 **Inside the Great Pyramid were two burial rooms, for the pharaoh and his queen.** The pharaoh's chamber was reached by a corridor called the Grand Gallery, with a roof more than 8 metres above the floor. Once the king's body was inside the chamber, the entrance was sealed with stone blocks. The last workers had to leave by specially built escape passages.

Western cemetery

Grand Gallery

Entrance

287 **The Great Sphinx at Giza guards the way to Khafre's pyramid.** It is a huge stone statue with the body of a lion and the head of a human.

▶ The features on the face of the Great Sphinx were carved to look like those of pharaoh Khafre.

288 **Tomb robbers broke into the pyramids to steal the fabulous treasures inside.** To make things difficult for the robbers, pyramid builders added heavy doors of granite and built false corridors.

289 **The earliest pyramids had stepped sides.** The steps were like a giant staircase, which the pharaoh could climb to reach the gods. The first step pyramid was built in the desert at Saqqara in about 2650 BC.

121

Supreme beings

290 The ancient Egyptians worshipped many gods and goddesses. The most important was Ra, the sun god. People believed that he was swallowed up each evening by the sky goddess Nut. During the night Ra travelled the underworld and was reborn each morning.

291 A god was often shown as an animal, or as half-human, half-animal. Bastet was goddess of cats, musicians and dancers. Cats were sacred in ancient Egypt. When a pet cat died, it was wrapped and laid in a cat-shaped coffin before burial in a cat cemetery. The moon god Thoth usually had the head of an ibis, but he was sometimes shown as a baboon. People believed that hieroglyphic writing came from Thoth.

Amun-Ra
Sun god

▶ Crocodiles were kept at the temples of the god Sobek.

Nut
Sky goddess

Sobek
God of the Nile

Bastet
Goddess of cats and music

◀ The sun god Ra was popular in Lower Egypt. The people of Upper Egypt linked him to their own god Amun, so both gods became known as Amun-Ra.

ANCIENT HISTORY

292 As god of the dead, Osiris was in charge of the underworld. Ancient Egyptians believed that dead people travelled to the kingdom of the underworld below the Earth. Osiris and his wife Isis were the parents of the god Horus, protector of the pharaoh.

293 Anubis was in charge of preparing bodies to be mummified. This work was known as embalming. Because jackals were often found near cemeteries, Anubis, who watched over the dead, was given the form of a jackal. Egyptian priests often wore Anubis masks.

294 Pharaoh Amenhotep IV worshipped one god – Aten the creator. He closed down temples to all other gods and even changed his name to Akhenaten, which means 'Spirit of Aten'.

Thoth
Moon god

Osiris
God of the underworld

Horus
God of the sky

Isis
Goddess of rebirth

Anubis
God of the dead

In tombs and temples

295 From about 2150 BC pharaohs were not buried in pyramids, but in tombs in the Valley of the Kings. This remote place was surrounded by steep cliffs on the west bank of the Nile opposite the city of Thebes. Some tombs were cut into the sides of the cliffs, others were built deep underground.

296 The riches in the tombs attracted robbers. The entrance to the Valley of the Kings was guarded, but robbers broke into every tomb except one within 1000 years. The only one they missed was the boy king Tutankhamun's, and even this had been partially robbed and re-sealed.

▼ Tutankhamun's sarcophagus was inside a set of four wooden shrines big enough to contain a modern car.

Outer wooden coffin
Middle wooden coffin
Inner gold coffin
Wrapped mummy
Inner coffin cover
Middle coffin cover
Outer coffin cover
Sarcophagus

297 Archaeologist Howard Carter discovered the tomb of Tutankhamun in 1922. An archaeologist is someone who studies ancient sites and objects. The body of Tutankhamun was found inside a nest of three mummy cases, encased within a sarcophagus (stone coffin).

ANCIENT HISTORY

I DON'T BELIEVE IT!
Temple visitors had to shave off their hair and eyebrows before they were allowed to enter the sacred buildings.

299 Building work at the Temples of Karnak lasted 1700 years from about 1900 BC. There were three great temples dedicated to the gods Amun-Re, Mut and Montu plus dozens of smaller temples and chapels. Today, millions of people flock to the area to see the remains of the once splendid temple structures.

298 **The Egyptians built fabulous temples to worship their gods.** Powerful priests ruled over the temples, and the riches and lands attached to them. Many of the finest temples were dedicated to Amun-Ra, king of the gods.

▼ The courtyard in the Temple of Amun-Re at Karnak was entered through a massive gateway, or pylon, about 17 metres tall.

Making mummies

300 **Making a mummy was skilled work.** First the brain, stomach, lungs and other organs were removed, but the heart was left in place. Next, the body was covered with salts and left to dry for up to 40 days. The dried body was washed and filled with linen and other stuffing to keep its shape. Then it was oiled and wrapped in linen bandages.

302 **Animals were made into mummies too.** A nobleman might be buried with a mummy of his pet cat. Mummification was expensive, so people only preserved animals in this way to offer them to the gods. One mummified crocodile discovered by archaeologists was over 4.5 metres long.

Canopic jars used to store organs

Priest wearing Anubis mask reads prayers

Amulets (charms) placed inside bandages

301 **Body parts were removed from the dead person and stored in special containers.** The stomach, intestines, lungs and liver were cut out and stored in four separate containers called canopic jars.

ANCIENT HISTORY

303 **A mask was fitted over the face of a mummy.** The ancient Egyptians believed that the mask would help the dead person's spirit to recognize the mummy later on. A pharaoh's mummy mask was made of gold and precious stones.

304 **When ready for burial, a mummy was placed inside a special case.** Some cases were simple wooden boxes, but others were shaped like mummies and richly decorated. The mummy case of an important person, such as a pharaoh or a nobleman, was sealed inside a stone coffin called a sarcophagus.

▼ The process of making mummies took place in sacred workshops and was accompanied by rituals and prayers.

It took many years of training to become a mummy-maker

Hundreds of metres of bandages were used

Clever Egyptians

305 The insides of many Egyptian tombs were decorated with brightly coloured wall paintings. The scenes showed what the Egyptians hoped life in the next world would be like.

▲ The Egyptians believed that these wall paintings would come to life in the next world.

306 Sculptors carved enormous statues of their pharaohs and gods. Stone statues up to 20 metres tall were placed outside tombs or temples to guard the entrance. Inside a tomb was a small wooden statue of the dead person where the ka, or life force, of the person could rest. Inside temples the holiest statue of a god would be made of silver, ivory or gold.

▲ Huge stone statues guard the entrance to the temple of Abu Simbel. When the temple was rediscovered in 1817, it was almost covered by sand.

ANCIENT HISTORY

307 **There were different calendars for different purposes.** A 365-day farming calendar was made up of three seasons of four months. An astronomical calendar was based on observations of the star Sirius, which reappeared at the start of the flood season. Priests kept a calendar based on the movements of the Moon, which told them when to perform ceremonies for the moon god.

308 **Nilometers were used to study the annual river floods.** As the water rose it entered a chamber marked with lines to measure the height of the flood and where priests could see how much mud the flood was bringing.

▼ The reappearance of Sirius in the night sky each summer marked the start of a new year and the oncoming floods. The Egyptian farming calendar had three seasons: flooding, planting and harvest.

309 **Astronomers recorded what they saw in the night skies.** They followed the movement of Sirius, the brightest star in the sky. The Egyptians used their knowledge of astronomy to build temples that lined up with certain stars.

310 **Egyptian doctors knew how to set broken bones and treat illnesses such as fevers.** They used medicines made from plants such as garlic and juniper to treat sick people. The Egyptians had a good knowledge of the basic workings of the human body.

From pictures to words

311 **The Egyptians had no paper – they wrote on papyrus.** It was made from papyrus reeds that grew on the banks of the Nile. At first papyrus was sold as long strips, or scrolls, tied with string. Later, papyrus sheets were put into books. Papyrus can last a very long time – sheets have survived 3000 years to the present day.

312 **Ink was made by mixing water with soot, charcoal or coloured minerals.** Scribes wrote in ink on papyrus scrolls, using reed brushes with specially shaped ends.

❶ Cutting
The papyrus stems were cut into lots of thin strips

❷ Laying
The strips were laid in rows on a frame to form layers

❸ Pressing
The strips were then pressed under weights to squeeze the water out and squash the layers together

❹ Rubbing
When the papyrus was dry, the surface was rubbed smooth for writing

▶ Egyptian papyrus was long-lasting because Egypt is such a hot, dry country.

ANCIENT HISTORY

313 The Rosetta Stone was found in 1799 by a French soldier in Egypt. It is a large stone onto which three kinds of writing have been carved: hieroglyphics, demotics (a simpler form of hieroglyphics), and Greek. All three sets of writing give an account of the coronation of King Ptolemy V.

▲ The Rosetta Stone in the British Museum. The stone itself is made of granite, and is a broken part of a bigger slab.

314 In the 5th century BC a Greek historian called Herodotus wrote about life in ancient Egypt. As he travelled across the country he observed and wrote about people's daily lives, and their religion and customs such as embalming and mummification.

▼ The name of Rameses II written inside a cartouche to show he was a pharaoh.

315 The hieroglyphs of a ruler's name were written inside an oval-shaped frame called a cartouche. The pharaoh's cartouche was carved on pillars and temple walls, painted on tomb walls and mummy cases, and written on official documents.

316 The Egyptians used a system of picture writing called hieroglyphics. Each hieroglyph represented an object or a sound. For example, the picture of a lion represented the sound 'l' and a basket represented the word 'lord'. There were around 700 different hierogylphs. Scribes wrote them on papyrus scrolls and advised stonemasons on how to carve them in temples and other buildings.

I DON'T BELIEVE IT!

Scribes were some of the most important people in ancient Egypt, as only they could write hieroglyphs. They began strict training at the age of nine.

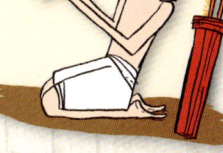

Greece was great

317 Ancient Greece was a small country, but its people had great ideas. From around 2000 BC, they created a splendid civilization that reached its peak between 500–400 BC. All citizens contributed to a society that respected people's rights and lived in harmony with the natural world. Today, we still admire Greek sport, politics, poetry and art.

▼ The Greeks' homeland included mainland Greece and over 2000 islands in the Aegean Sea and the Ionian Sea, together with the coast of Asia Minor.

318 Greek civilization began on the islands. Some of the first evidence of farming in Greece comes from the Cyclades Islands. Around 6000 BC, people living there began to plant grain and build villages.

▼ This timeline shows some of the important events in the history of ancient Greece.

TIMELINE OF GREECE

c. 40,000 BC First people in Greece. They are hunters and gatherers

c. 2000–1450 BC Minoan civilization on the island of Crete

c. 1250 BC Traditional date of the Trojan War

c. 900–700 BC Greek civilization grows strong again

c. 6000 BC First farmers in Greece

c. 1600–1100 BC Mycenean civilization on mainland Greece

c. 1100–900 BC A time of decline – kingdoms weaken, writing stops

c. 776 BC Traditional date of first Olympic Games

ANCIENT HISTORY

319 **Between 1100–900 BC, the history of Greece is a mystery.** From 2000–1100 BC, powerful kings ruled Greece. They left incredible buildings and objects behind them, and used writing. But between around 1100–900 BC, there were no strong kingdoms, little art, few new buildings – and writing disappeared.

320 **Migrants settled in distant lands.** By around 700 BC, Greece was overcrowded. There were too many people, not enough farmland to grow food and some islands were short of water. Greek families left to set up colonies far away, from southern France to North Africa, Turkey and Bulgaria.

321 **When the neighbours invaded, Greek power collapsed.** After 431 BC, Greek cities were at war and the fighting weakened them. In 338 BC, Philip II of Macedonia (a kingdom north of Greece) invaded with a large army. After Philip died, his son, Alexander the Great, made Greece part of his mighty empire.

c. 700–500 BC
Greeks set up colonies around Mediterranean Sea

c. 480–479 BC
Greece fights invaders from Persia (now Iran)

c. 338 BC
Philip II of Macedonia conquers Greece

c. 147–146 BC
Romans conquer Greece and Macedonia

c. 500–430 BC
Athens leads Greece, creates amazing art, has democratic government

c. 431–404 BC
Wars between Athens and Sparta

c. 336–323 BC
Alexander the Great of Macedonia and Greece conquers a vast empire

Kings and warriors

322 **King Minos ruled an amazing palace-city.** The first great Greek civilization grew up at Knossos on the island of Crete. Historians call it 'Minoan' after its legendary king, Minos. Around 2000 BC, Minoan kings built an amazing palace-city, with rooms for 10,000 people. It was decorated with wonderful frescoes (wall paintings), statues and pottery.

▲ A section of the palace at Knossos on the island of Crete. A succession of powerful kings ruled a rich kingdom here.

323 **Minoan Greeks honoured a monster.** Greek myths describe how a fearsome monster was kept in a labyrinth (underground maze) below the palace. It was called the Minotaur, and it was half-man, half-bull.

▲ Greek legends told how the young hero Theseus bravely entered the labyrinth and killed the Minotaur.

ANCIENT HISTORY

QUIZ

1. What was the Minotaur?
2. What was the labyrinth?
3. Where was Knossos?

Answers:
1. A monster – half-man, half-bull 2. A maze underneath the Minoan royal palace 3. On the Greek island of Crete

Oule = Hello

Khaire = Goodbye

▶ This golden mask was found in one of the royal tombs at Mycenae. It covered the face of a king who died around 1500 BC.

324 **Invaders brought the Greek language.** Between around 2100–1700 BC, warriors from the north arrived in mainland Greece. They brought new words with them and their language was copied by everyone else living in Greece.

325 **Mycenae was ruled by warrior kings.** Around 1600 BC new kings took control of Minoan lands from forts on the Greek mainland. The greatest fort was at Mycenae, in the far south of Greece. Mycenaean kings sent traders to Egypt and the Near East to exchange Greek pottery and olive oil for gold, tin and amber. They used their wealth to pay for huge tombs in which they were buried.

▼ Works of art found at Knossos include many images of huge, fierce bulls with athletes leaping between their horns in a deadly religious ritual.

135

City-states

326 The power of Mycenaean kings collapsed around 1200 BC. By 700 BC, Greece had been divided into 300 city-states, which were cities and the land around them. Some city-states were ruled by kings, some by tyrants (men who governed by force) and some by oligarchs (small groups of rich, powerful men).

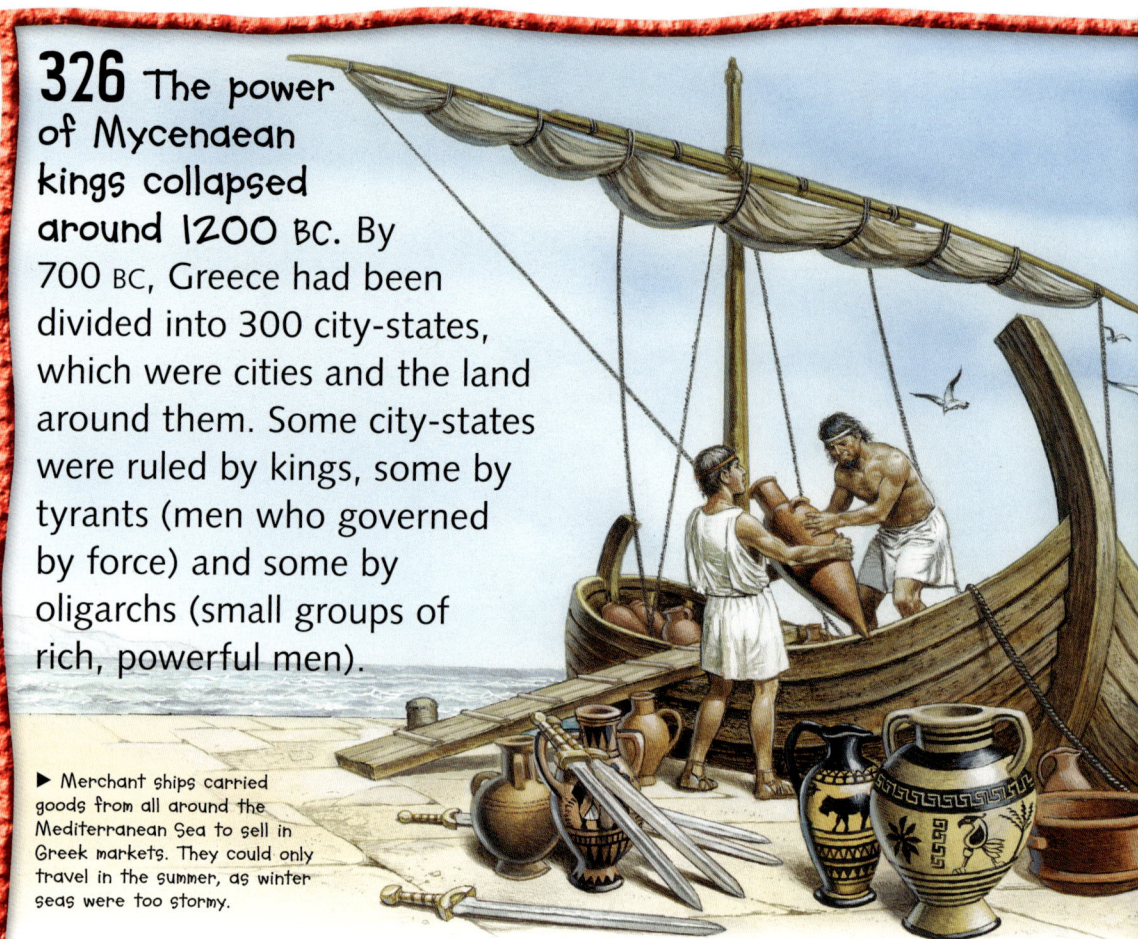

▶ Merchant ships carried goods from all around the Mediterranean Sea to sell in Greek markets. They could only travel in the summer, as winter seas were too stormy.

327 Most city-states grew rich by buying and selling. The agora (market-place) was the centre of many cities. Goods on sale included farm produce such as grain, wine and olive oil, salt from the sea, pottery, woollen blankets, sheepskin cloaks, leather sandals and even people.

328 Top craftsmen made fine goods for sale. Cities were home to many expert craftsmen. They ran small workshops next to their homes, or worked as slaves in factories owned by rich businessmen. Greek craftworkers were famous for producing fine pottery, stone-carvings, weapons, armour and jewellery.

ANCIENT HISTORY

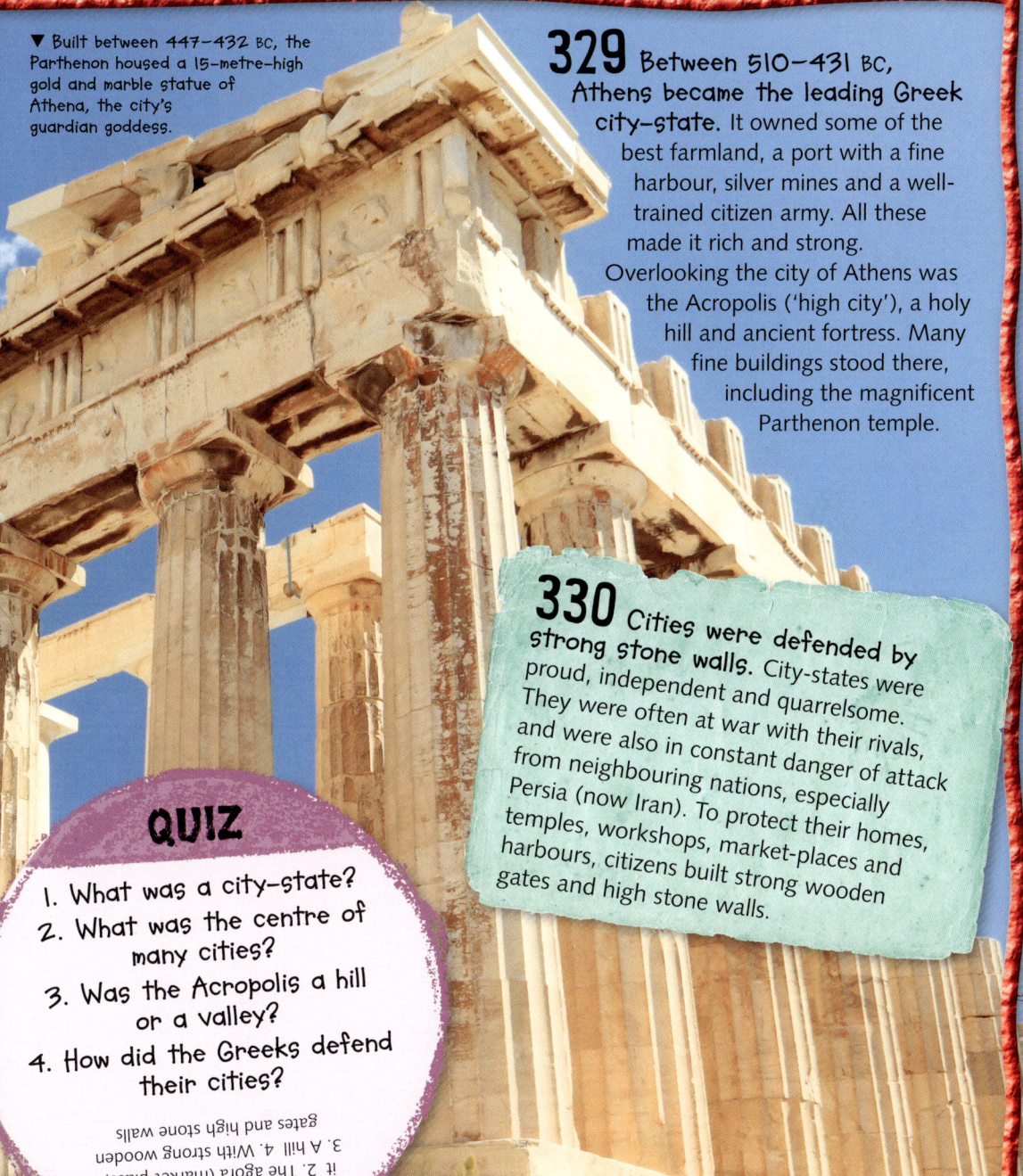

▼ Built between 447–432 BC, the Parthenon housed a 15-metre-high gold and marble statue of Athena, the city's guardian goddess.

329 **Between 510–431 BC, Athens became the leading Greek city-state.** It owned some of the best farmland, a port with a fine harbour, silver mines and a well-trained citizen army. All these made it rich and strong. Overlooking the city of Athens was the Acropolis ('high city'), a holy hill and ancient fortress. Many fine buildings stood there, including the magnificent Parthenon temple.

330 **Cities were defended by strong stone walls.** City-states were proud, independent and quarrelsome. They were often at war with their rivals, and were also in constant danger of attack from neighbouring nations, especially Persia (now Iran). To protect their homes, temples, workshops, market-places and harbours, citizens built strong wooden gates and high stone walls.

QUIZ

1. What was a city-state?
2. What was the centre of many cities?
3. Was the Acropolis a hill or a valley?
4. How did the Greeks defend their cities?

Answers:
1. A city and the land around it 2. The agora (market-place) 3. A hill 4. With strong wooden gates and high stone walls

Gods and goddesses

331 To the Greeks, the world was full of dangers and disasters that they could not understand or control. There were also many good things, such as love, joy, music and beauty, that were wonderful but mysterious. The Greeks thought of all these unknown forces as gods and goddesses who shaped human life and ruled the world.

▶ This statue of the goddess Aphrodite was carved from white marble — a very smooth, delicate stone. It was designed to portray the goddess' perfect beauty. Sadly, it has been badly damaged over the centuries.

▶ Poseidon was god of the sea and storms. He also sent terrifying earthquakes to punish people — or cities — that offended him.

332 Gods and goddesses were pictured as superhuman creatures. They were strong and very beautiful. However, like humans, gods and goddesses also had weaknesses. Aphrodite was thoughtless, Hera was jealous, Apollo and his sister Artemis were cruel, and Ares was bad-tempered.

ANCIENT HISTORY

333 The Greeks believed in magic spirits and monsters. These included Gorgons who turned men to stone, and Sirens – bird-women whose song lured sailors to their doom. They also believed in witchcraft and curses and tried to fight against them. People painted magic eyes on the prows of their ships to keep a look-out for evil.

▲ Odysseus and his shipmates were surrounded by the Sirens – beautiful half-women, half-bird monsters. They sang sweet songs, calling sailors towards dangerous rocks where their ships were wrecked.

334 Individuals were often anxious to see what the future would bring. They believed that oracles (holy messengers) could see the future. The most famous oracles were at Delphi, where a drugged priestess answered questions, and at Dodona, where the leaves of sacred trees whispered words from the gods.

▶ Herakles was a hero – a man who became a god. He performed amazing feats of strength and fought against many monsters. This statue shows him killing a centaur, half-man, half-horse.

335 Poets and dramatists retold myths and legends about the gods. Some stories were explanations of natural events – thunder was the god Zeus shaking his fist in anger. Others explored bad thoughts and feelings shared by gods and humans, such as greed and disloyalty.

139

War on land and sea

336 **As teenagers, all Greek male citizens were trained to fight.** They had to be ready to defend their city whenever danger threatened. City-states also employed men as bodyguards and mercenary troops with special skills.

▼▶ Soldiers had different duties. Cavalrymen were messengers and spies. Peltasts had to move fast and were armed with javelins. Mercenaries fought for anyone who would pay them.

Peltast

Hoplite

Cavalry

Mercenary

337 **Each soldier paid for his own weapons and armour.** Most soldiers were hoplites (soldiers who fought on foot). Their most important weapons were swords and spears. Poor men could not afford swords or armour. The only weapons they had were slings for shooting stones and simple wooden spears.

338 **Soldiers rarely fought on horseback.** At the start of a battle, hoplites lined up side by side with their shields overlapping, like a wall. Then they marched towards the enemy while the peltasts threw their javelins. When they were close enough, the hoplites used their spears to fight the enemy.

◀ A Corinthian-style helmet. Soldiers tried to protect themselves from injury with bronze helmets, breastplates, greaves (shin guards) and round wooden shields.

ANCIENT HISTORY

I DON'T BELIEVE IT!

Ancient Greek soldiers rarely rode horses — because stirrups had not yet been invented. Without stirrups to support him, a soldier on horseback who hurled a spear or stabbed with a sword was likely to fall off backwards!

339 City-states paid for fleets of fast, fearsome wooden warships, called triremes. Each ship had a crew of about 170 oarsmen who sat in three sets of seats, one above the other. They rowed the ship as fast as they could towards enemy vessels, hoping that the sharp, pointed ram at its prow would smash or sink them. The most famous naval battle in Greece was fought at Salamis, near Athens, in 480 BC, when the Greeks defeated the Persians.

▼ Greek ships were made of wood. If they were holed below the waterline they sank very quickly.

141

Olympic Games

340 **The Olympic Games began as a festival to honour Zeus.** Over the centuries, it grew into the greatest sports event in the Greek world. A huge festival complex was built at Olympia with a temple, sports tracks, seats for 40,000 spectators, a campsite and rooms for visitors and a field full of stalls selling food and drink.

▶ Victory! The Greeks believed that winners were chosen by the gods. The first known Olympic Games was held in 776 BC, though the festival may have begun years earlier.

341 Every four years athletes travelled from all over Greece to take part in the Olympic Games. They had to obey strict rules – respect for Zeus, no fights among competitors and no weapons anywhere near the sports tracks. In return they claimed protection – the holy Olympic Peace. Anyone who attacked them on their journeys was severely punished.

QUIZ

1. When were the first Olympic Games held?
2. Could women take part in the Olympic Games?
3. What did winning athletes wear on their heads?

Answers:
1. 776 BC, though the festival may have begun years earlier 2. No. There was a separate women's games held 3. Crowns of holy laurel leaves

ANCIENT HISTORY

▲ Boxers did not wear gloves. Instead they wrapped their hands in bandages.

342 **The most popular events were running, long jump, wrestling and boxing.** Spectators might also watch chariot races, athletes throwing the discus and javelin or weightlifting contests. The most prestigious event was the 200-metre sprint. There was also a dangerous fighting contest called *pankration* (total power).

343 **Many events featured weapons or skills that were needed in war.** One of the most gruelling competitions was a race wearing heavy battle armour. The main Olympic Games were for men only – women could not take part. There was a separate women's games held at Olympia on different years from the men's competitions.

▲ Throwing the discus was a test of strength and balance. It was also useful training for war.

▲ Swimmer Michael Phelps sets a new world record at the Beijing Olympics, 2008. The modern Olympics is modelled on the ancient games and since 1896 has remained the world's greatest sports festival.

344 **Athletes who won Olympic contests were honoured as heroes.** They were crowned with wreaths of holy laurel leaves and given valuable prizes of olive oil, fine clothes and pottery. Poets composed songs in their praise and their home city-states often rewarded them with free food and lodgings for life!

▶ A crown of laurel leaves was given to winning athletes as a sign of their god-like strength and speed.

The heart of Rome

345 **The Italian city of Rome was once the hub of one of the world's greatest empires.** By around AD 300, it was the largest city in the world. There were citizens who could vote and serve in the army, and there were non-citizens who did not have these rights. The government was run by wealthy nobles and knights. Plebeians (ordinary people) were usually fairly poor but were citizens of Rome. Slaves were non-citizens. They were not free to leave their owners and had no rights.

▼ In 44 BC the dictator Julius Caesar built the Curia Julia as a meeting house for the Senate of Rome. The building later became a church and has survived intact to the present day.

346 **The Forum was the centre of Rome.** It was originally an open space at the foot of the Capitoline Hill, and was used as a market place, meeting place and picnic area. Later, government buildings were erected here, including offices for the Senate, law courts and temples.

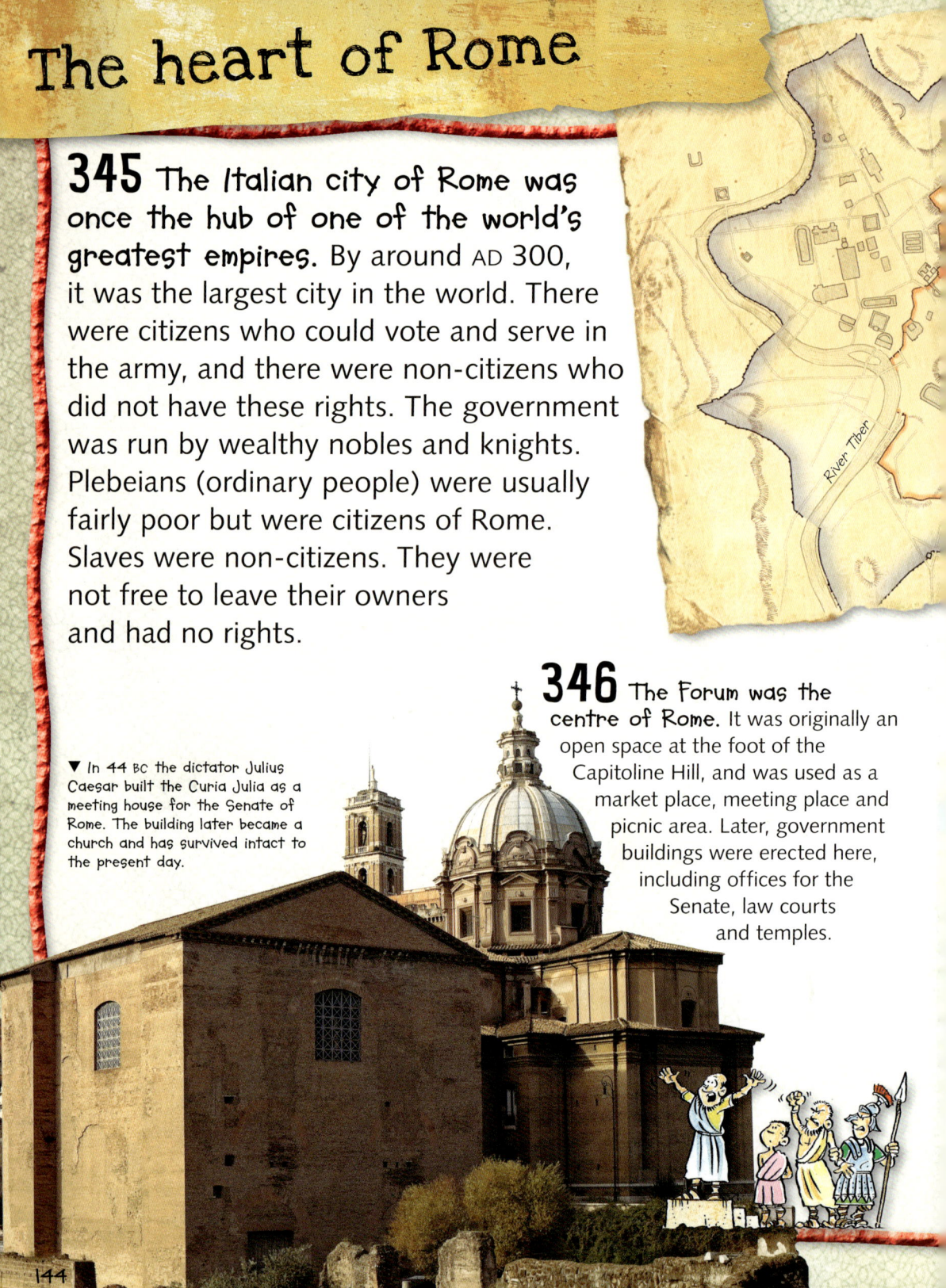

ANCIENT HISTORY

347 **Rome was very well protected.** It was surrounded by 50 kilometres of strong stone walls to keep out attackers. Visitors had to enter the city through one of its 37 gates, which were guarded by soldiers and watchmen.

◀ In AD 275 the old Servian Wall of about 380 BC was replaced by the Aurelian Wall that protected the new, larger city of Rome. The new wall was 19 kilometres long, 16 metres tall and had 383 towers. It remained in use until the siege of 1870.

348 **The Romans were great water engineers.** They designed aqueducts (raised channels to carry water from streams in distant hills and mountains to the city). The homes of rich citizens were supplied with running water carried in lead pipes. Ordinary people had to drink from public fountains.

349 **Rome relied on its drains.** The city was so crowded that without good drains the citizens could have caught diseases from sewage and died. The largest sewer, called the *cloaca maxima*, was so high and wide that a horse and cart could drive through it.

I DON'T BELIEVE IT!
Roman engineers also designed public lavatories. They were convenient but not at all private – users had to sit on rows of seats, side by side!

▶ The Romans built the Pont Du Gard in the south of France – a 360-metre-long aqueduct supported on three tiers of arches.

Home sweet home

▲ A reconstruction of a house belonging to a rich family in the city of Pompeii. This grand room, the Atrium, was where guests were entertained.

QUIZ
1. What were Roman blocks of flats known as?
2. What are pictures made with coloured stones or glass called?
3. How did Romans heat their homes?

Answers:
1. Insulae 2. Mosaics 3. Wealthy families had underfloor heating, ordinary families used fires

350 Rich Romans had more than one home. Rome was noisy, dirty and smelly. Wealthy citizens would often have a house just outside the city (a *villa urbana*), or a big house with land in the country (a *villa rustica*) in which they spent the summer months.

ANCIENT HISTORY

351 **The Romans built the world's first high-rise apartments.** Most of the people who lived in Ostia, a busy port close to Rome, had jobs connected with trade, such as shipbuilders and money-changers. They lived in blocks of flats known as *insulae*. A typical block was three or four storeys high, with up to 100 small, dirty, crowded rooms.

353 **Many homes had a pool, but it wasn't used for swimming!** Decorative pools were built in the central courtyards of large homes, surrounded by plants and statues. Some had fountains. In others mosaics (pictures made of tiny coloured stones or squares of glass) covered the floor.

▼ On the ground floor of an *insula* were shops, and on the first floor were flats and apartments for families. The poorest families lived in single rooms on the top floor.

354 **Rome's fire brigade was made up of specially trained freed slaves.** People who could not afford central heating warmed their rooms with fires in clay pots, which often set houses alight.

352 **Wealthy family homes had underfloor central heating.** Blasts of hot air, warmed by a wood-burning furnace, circulated in channels built beneath the floor. Slaves chopped wood and stoked the fire.

▶ Some public buildings and wealthy homes had a heating system called a hypocaust. Hot air from a fire tended by a slave passed through spaces under the floor and up the walls to keep the rooms warm.

Space in walls for hot air to circulate

Fire in basement

Space under floor for hot air to circulate

147

Bath time

▼ The Roman baths at Bath, in Somerset. Only the actual water bath is original, the other buildings date from the 18th century.

355 The Romans went to public baths to relax. These huge buildings were more than just places to get clean. They were also fitness centres and meeting places. Visitors could take part in sports, such as wrestling, do exercises, have a massage or a haircut. They could buy scented oils and perfumes, read books, eat snacks or admire works of art in the bath's own sculpture gallery!

356 Men and women could not bathe together. Women usually went to the baths in the mornings, while most men were at work. Men went to the baths in the afternoons.

I DON'T BELIEVE IT!
Although the Romans liked bathing, they visited the baths only once in every nine days. Basins of water were used in between baths to wash hands or faces.

ANCIENT HISTORY

357 Bathing wasn't simple – there were lots of stages. First bathers sat in a very hot room full of steam. Then they went into a hot, dry room, where a slave removed all the sweat and dirt from their skin, using a metal scraper and olive oil. To cool off, they went for a swim in a tepid pool. Finally, they jumped into a bracing cold pool.

▼ The Baths of Caracalla in Rome included not only baths but libraries, shops and gardens that covered a total of 25 hectares.

❶ *Tepidarium* Cool or tepid pool

❷ *Caldarium* Hot room

Frigidarium Coldest pool

Fires heat the water for the hot rooms

▲ Roman baths were open to anyone who paid the entrance fee. They were one of the few areas where rich and poor mixed freely. Some baths had two sections, one for men and one for women, but most baths had days for men and days for women.

149

Let the games begin

358 Gladiators were admired for their strength, skill and bravery. These men were sent into an arena (an open space with tiered seats on all sides) to fight. Most gladiators would be killed or badly injured in the arena.

▶ Different types of gladiator had special equipment and fought in ways governed by strict rules, which were enforced by a referee.

Secutor

Samnite

Hoplomachus

359 Most gladiators didn't choose to fight. They were prisoners of war or criminals condemned to fight in the arena. Some men volunteered as gladiators to gain fame and wealth. Success could bring riches and freedom.

I DON'T BELIEVE IT!
Some gladiators became so popular that people used to write graffiti about them on the walls of buildings around Rome!

360 Gladiators fought wild beasts. Animals such as lions, tigers and crocodiles were brought from distant parts of the Empire to be hunted by gladiators in the arena. Sometimes criminals with no weapons were put into the arena along with the wild animals. They did not last long.

361 The Colosseum was an amazing building for its time. Also known as the Flavian Amphitheatre, it was a huge oval arena in the centre of Rome, used for gladiator fights and the executions of criminals. It opened in AD 80, and could seat 50,000 people. It was built of stone, concrete and marble and had 80 separate entrances.

▼ The Colosseum was the largest amphitheatre in the Roman empire.

▶ Chariot drivers wore helmets, but no other protective clothing.

362 Some Romans liked a day at the races. Horses pulled fast chariots round racetracks, called 'circuses'. The most famous was the Circus Maximus in Rome, which could hold 250,000 spectators. There could be up to 24 races each day. Twelve chariots took part in each race, running seven times round the oval track – a total distance of about 8 kilometres.

363 Chariots often collided and overturned. Each charioteer carried a sharp knife, called a *falx*, to cut himself free from the wreckage. Even so, many horses and charioteers were killed.

364 Racing rivalries sometimes led to riots. Races were organized by four separate teams – the Reds, Blues, Greens and Whites. Charioteers wore tunics in their team colours. Each team had a keen – and violent – group of fans.

Ruling Rome

365 According to legend, the first king, Romulus, came to power in 753 BC. Six kings ruled after him, but they were unjust and cruel. After King Tarquin the Proud was overthrown in 509 BC Rome became a republic (a state without a king). Every year the people elected two consuls (senior lawyers) to head the government. Other officials were elected too. The republic lasted for over 400 years.

▼ Caesar's power and ambition angered his political opponents, and a group of them assassinated him.

366 In 47 BC a successful general called Julius Caesar declared himself dictator. This meant that he wanted to rule on his own for life. Many people feared that he was trying to end the republic, and rule like the old kings. Caesar was murdered in 44 BC by his political enemies. After this, there were many years of civil war.

▲ Legend says the twins Romulus and Remus were suckled by a wolf before being rescued by a shepherd.

I DON'T BELIEVE IT!
Some Roman emperors were mad and even dangerous. Emperor Nero was said to have laughed and played music while watching a terrible fire that destroyed a large part of Rome.

▲ This fresco shows the emperor Trajan with his army around AD 106. By this date emperors would command the army in battle and were expected to be talented generals.

367 In 27 BC Caesar's nephew Octavian seized power in Rome. He declared himself 'First Citizen', and said he would bring back peace and good government to Rome. He ended the civil war, and introduced many strong new laws. But he also changed the Roman government forever. He took a new name, 'Augustus', and became the first emperor of Rome.

368 Later the army took over. In AD 193 Emperor Commodus was murdered and the senate met to decide who would take over. The army marched to Rome and made Septimus Severus emperor. After this it was the army who decided who would be emperor.

Emperor Caligula
AD 12–41

Emperor Nero
AD 37–68

Emperor Constantine
280–337

◀ The emperors put their portraits on coins to remind everyone who was in charge of the empire.

◀ The Roman general Octavian Caesar ruled Rome from 27 BC to AD 14.

Ruled by Rome

369 More than 50 million people were ruled by Rome. Celts, Germans, Iberians, and many other peoples lived in territories held by Rome's armies. They had their own languages, customs and beliefs. Rome sent governors to force conquered peoples to pay taxes and obey Roman laws.

▼ The Roman city of Londinium (London) was built at a point where the wide River Thames could be bridged.

370 A few conquered kings and queens did not accept Roman rule. In AD 60 Boudicca, queen of the Iceni tribe of eastern England, led a rebellion against the Romans in Britain. Her army marched on London and other cities but was defeated by Roman soldiers.

▼ British warriors led by Queen Boudicca destroyed cities and killed everyone they found.

I DON'T BELIEVE IT!
Roman soldiers guarding the cold northern frontiers of Britain kept warm by wearing short woollen trousers – like underpants – beneath their tunics!

ANCIENT HISTORY

371 Cleopatra used beauty and charm to stop the Romans invading. Cleopatra was queen of Egypt and she knew that the Egyptian army would not be able to defeat Roman soldiers. Two Roman army generals, Julius Caesar and Mark Antony, fell in love with Cleopatra. She prevented the Romans invading for many years, but Egypt was eventually conquered.

▶ Queen Cleopatra shown wearing the traditional clothing of an Egyptian queen.

▼ This map shows the Roman Empire in brown, and the roads that they built in black.

372 Romans built monuments to celebrate their victories. Trajan, who ruled from AD 98–117, was a Roman soldier who became emperor. After his army conquered Dacia (now Romania) in AD 106, he gave orders for a 30-metre-high stone pillar to be built in the Forum in Rome. The pillar was decorated with carvings of 2500 Roman soldiers winning wars. It still stands today and is known as Trajan's Column.

155

INDEX

A
Acropolis 137
air 4, 14, 33, 66–67
Alexander the Great 133
Allosaurus 92, 93
aluminium 59
alveoli 66, 67
Amazon river 20
amphibians 98, 108–109
ancient history 116–155
animals 25, 26–27, 96–115, 122, 126, 150
Antarctica 23, 29
antennae 101, 112, 113
ants 113
Anubis 123
aqueducts 145
arachnids 114–115
archaeologists 124
Arctic 28
arteries 72
asteroids 8, 9
astronauts 4, 5
astronomers 129
Athens 137
atmosphere 4, 12, 13, 14, 15, 32–33, 35
atoms 46–47, 52, 54, 58, 59
auroras 15, 32
axis of Earth 28

B
bacteria 69, 71
baths, Roman 148–149
batteries 54
beetles 112, 113
birds 98, 99, 103, 106–107
bladder 73
blood 66, 72–73, 74–75, 81
blood vessels 63, 66, 68, 72–73, 74, 75
bone marrow 63
bones 62–63, 64–65, 99
Boudicca 154
brain 62, 76, 77, 78, 79, 80, 81, 82–83, 98
breathing 66–67, 109, 111

burials 120, 121, 124–125, 126, 127
burning 48, 49, 55
butterflies 112

C
Caesar, Julius 152–153, 155
calendars, Egyptian 129
capillaries 72
carbon 47, 59
carbon dioxide 14, 28, 66, 72
cardiac muscle 74
cartilage 62
cartouche 131
cerebellum 82, 83
cerebral cortex 82
cerebrum 82
Challenger Deep 30
chariot races 151
chemicals 49, 54
circulatory system 72–73, 74–75
city-states 136–137, 140–141
claws 84, 85, 86, 90–91, 103
Cleopatra 155
cliffs 17
clouds 13, 22, 23, 32, 34–35, 36
cochlea 77
collagen 63, 64
Colosseum 151
colour spectrum 50
comets 9
computers 56–57
conduction 48
coniferous forests 24
continental drift 18
convection 49
cornea 76
coronary vessels 75
craters 13
crust of Earth 12, 14, 16, 18
cyclones 38

D
Deinonychus 90
deserts 22–23, 41
diamonds 59

diaphragm 67
digestive system 70–71
dinosaurs 84–95
Diplodocus 88, 89

E
ears 77, 94, 100, 102
Earth 4–9, 12–43
  formation of 12–13
  layers of 14
  tilt of 15
earwigs 112
eclipses 7
Egypt, ancient 20, 116–131, 155
electricity 53, 54–55
electromagnets 53
electrons 46, 47, 52, 54
elements 46, 58–59
enzymes 70
evolution 85
eyes 76–77, 82, 94, 100

F
faeces 71
feathers 90, 91, 106
fish 98, 99, 110–111
flies 112, 113
floods 42–43, 117, 129
forests 24–27
fossil fuels 55
frogs 98, 99, 109

G
galaxies 4, 10–11
gases 4, 6, 12, 13, 14, 15, 49, 55, 58, 59
gills 111
gladiators 150, 151
glands 60, 81, 104, 109
glass 49, 50, 51
global warming 28, 31, 39, 43
gods and goddesses 122–123, 125, 129, 137, 138–139
gravity 8, 12, 33
Great Pyramid 120–121
Greece, ancient 132–143

INDEX

H
hailstones 37
hearing 77, 82, 94, 100, 102
heart 72–73, 74–75, 98
heat 33, 48–49, 147
Herodotus 131
hieroglyphics 122, 131
hoplites 140
hormones 72, 81
human body 44, 60–83
hurricanes 38–39
hydrogen 46, 58
hydrothermal vents 31

I
Iguanodon 91
insects 98, 100, 101, 112–113, 114
insulae 147
International Space Station 5, 15, 32
invertebrates 98
iron 15, 52, 53, 58

J
joints 62, 63
Jupiter 8

K
keratin 60, 90, 106, 108
Khufu, King 120
kidneys 73
Knossos 134, 135

L
labyrinth 134
ladybirds 112
large intestine 71
lemmings 105
lenses 51, 76
ligaments 62
light 50–51
lightning 36–37
liver 71
Londinium 154–155
lungs 66–67

M
magnetic field 15, 52, 53
magnetism 52–53
mammals 98, 99, 100, 104–105
mantle 14, 18, 19
Mariana Trench 30
marrow 63
Mars 8, 9
marsupials 105
mercenaries 140
Mercury 8, 9
metal 15, 46, 48, 51, 52, 54, 59
meteorites 12, 13
microchips 56, 57
Milky Way 10, 11
Minoan lands 134, 135
mirrors 50, 51
mites 114, 115
molecules 33, 48, 59
monotremes 104
Moon, Earth's 5, 7, 9, 13, 129
moons 4, 9
mosaics 147
motor nerve signals 80
mountains 13, 16–17, 31, 33, 34
mummification 123, 126–127
muscles 64–65, 67, 70, 74, 76, 79, 83
Mycenae 135, 136

N
nanotechnology 47
Neptune 8
nerve cells 76, 81
nerve signals 76–77, 78–79, 80, 82
nerves 80–81
neutrons 46, 47
Nile river 20, 42, 116–117, 124, 129
North Pole 15, 28–29
nose 78, 101
nucleus 46, 47

O
oases 23
oceans 13, 14, 18, 28, 30–31, 34, 35, 38, 39, 97
Octavian 153
oesophagus 69
olfactory cells 78–79
Olympic Games 132, 142–143
optics 50–51
Osiris 123
oxygen 14, 33, 46, 49, 66–67, 72, 74

P
pancreas 71, 81
Pangaea 19
papillae 79
papyrus 130
Parasaurolophus 95
Parthenon 137
penguins 28–29
Periodic Table 58–59
Persia (Iran) 133, 137, 141
pharaohs 118–119, 127, 131
Philip II, King 133
pituitary gland 81
planets 4, 8–9, 12
plants 23, 25, 26–27
plate boundaries 18, 19
Plateosaurus 86
poles 15, 28–29, 52–53
pollution 28, 55,
predators 89, 92–93, 102–103
prey 102–103
prisms 50
protons 46, 47
pyramids 120–121

R
Ra 122
radiation 4, 48
radioactivity 59
rain 20, 22, 23, 26, 34–35, 42
rainforests 20, 25, 26–27, 96
  layers 25, 27
Rameses II 119, 131
reflection 50
refraction 51

INDEX

reptiles 85, 87, 94, 98, 99, 108–109
republic of Rome 152
respiratory system 66–67
retina 76
Riojasaurus 87
rivers 20–21, 34, 42, 117, 129
Roman Empire 154–155
Romans 116, 133, 144–155
Rosetta Stone 131

S

Sahara Desert 22
sand dunes 22, 23
Saturn 8
sauropods 88–89, 91
science 44–83
scorpions 115
sea levels 31, 43
seas 13, 41, 42
senses 76–77, 78–79, 82, 100–101, 105
sensory nerve signals 80
sharks 103, 110–111
ships 136, 139, 141
sight 76–77, 82, 94, 100
silk 114
skeletal muscles 64
skeleton 62–63, 99
skin 60–61, 65, 109
small intestine 70, 71
smell 78–79, 94–95, 101, 105
solar flares 6, 7
solar system 8–9
solar wind 15
South Pole 15, 28–29
space 4–15, 32
spiders 103, 114–115
spinal cord 83
sponges 97
stars 4, 6–7, 10–11, 12, 58, 129
steel 52
stomach 70, 71
storms 36–37, 38–39
Sun 6–9, 12, 14–15, 33, 48
supernovae 12

T

tails 84, 86, 88, 89, 110, 111
taste 79, 82, 101
tectonic plates 18, 19
teeth 68–69, 84, 85, 89, 93
temperate forests 24, 25
temperature 49, 61
temples 123, 124–125, 128, 129, 131, 137, 142, 144
tendons 64
therizinosaurs 91
Thoth 122, 123
thresher sharks 111
thunderstorms 36–37, 40
thyroid gland 81
tombs 120–121, 124–125, 128, 135
tongue 79, 101, 102, 103
tornadoes 40–41
touch 60, 61, 82, 101
Trajan's Column 155
trees 24–27
triremes 141
Troodon 94, 95
tropical forests 24, 25
troposphere 32, 33
Tutankhamun 124
typhoons 38
Tyrannosaurus rex 92, 93

U

uranium 59
Uranus 8
urine 73

V

valves 75
veins 72
Venus 8, 9
vertebrates 99, 101
virga 35
volcanoes 12, 13, 18–19

W Z

water 13, 14, 20, 23, 28, 34, 35, 41, 42, 43, 49, 51
water cycle 34–35
water supply 43, 117, 145
waterfalls 20, 21
weapons 140, 143, 150
weather 32, 33, 34–41
white light 50
winds 38, 40
wings 106
Zeus 139

ACKNOWLEDGEMENTS

All artworks are from the Miles Kelly Artwork Bank

The publishers would like to thank the following sources for the use of their photographs:
(t = top, b = bottom, l = left, r = right, c = centre, bg = background)

Alamy 16(br) Granger; 20(bl) Prisma Bildagentur AG; 23(br) Avalon/World Pictures; 25(tr) Michael & Patricia Fogden/Minden Pictures; 26(bg) imageBROKER; 29(b) Minden Pictures; 35(br) Yva Momatiuk & John Eastcott/Minden Pictures; 42(b) Mike Goldwater; 43(tr) Darren Staples; 84(tr) agefotostock; 85(cr) dpa picture alliance archive; 88(bl) Ida Pap; 144(b) Agencja Fotograficzna Caro; 146(tl) PhotoStock-Israel; 152(bl) Universal Images Group North America LLC/DeAgostini

Avalon 103(bc) Mike Lane/Woodfall

Diomedia 135(tr) DeAgostini/A. PISTOLESI

Dreamstime 50(bg) Theo Gottwald; 51(l) Adam Gryko; 59(br) Alan Heartfield; 69(tr) Kati1313; 98(fish) Olga Khoroshunova; 114(bg) Cathy Keifer

Ecoscene 37(bl) Nick Hawkes

FLPA 24(bg) Phil McLean; 102(bg) Elliott Neep

Fotolia 6(graph paper, used throughout) Sharpshot; 16(bl) QiangBa DanZhen; 21(tl) Albo; 65(tr) Alexander Y; 77(talking) Andres Rodriguez; 98(reptile) Paul Murphy, 98(amphibian) Audrey Snider-Bell; 115(bg) noyiil; 116(paper, used throughout) Alexey Khromushin; 119(br, paper) Rafa Irusta

Glow 128(b) Newberry Library

iStock 23(tl) pkruger; 38(b) dswebb; 124(bl) Duncan P Walker; 139(br) Danilo Ascione; 140(bc) Keith Binns; 143(tl) Brigida Soriano, (br) redmal

Nasa 6(bl) JPL, (bc) Goddard Space Flight Center Scientific Visualization Studio, (tl); 7(cl); 8(bg) JPL; 11(tr) STScI, (tl) Chandra X-ray Observatory Center, (cl) ESA and the Hubble Heritage (STScI_AURA)–ESA_Hubble Collaboration), (bl) ESA and A. Nota (STScI/ESA); 15(b) Space Station; 32(bl) JPL/UCSD/JSC; 42(tr) GSFC/JPL, MISR Team

Science Photo Library 12(bg) Richard Bizley; 13(bg) Mark Garlick; 37(cr) Peter Menzel; 47(bc) Victor Habbick Visions (Old Laguna Design); 88(bg) Julius T Csotonyi; 89(bg) Sciepro; 91(br) Jose Antonio Penas

ShutterstockPremier 7(cl) Dimec; 10(bg) John A Davis; 13(tr) godrick; 14(tr) Seadam; 15(t) nuttakit; 17(bg) Celso Diniz; 21(r) Vadim Petrakov; 25(cl) Steve Bower; 29(tr) TravelMediaProductions; 33(bg) Taras Kushnir; 34(bl) Alexandr Zyryanov; 36–37(bg) kornilov007; 37(tl) Jack Dagley Photography, (cr) Gunnar Pippel; 38(t) Roypix; 40–41(bg) Justin Hobson; 44(bg) ssguy; 48(bl) Ivonne Wierink, (tr) Pavel Vakhrushev; 48–49(bg) DeymosHR; 49(t) W Shane Dougherty; 52–53 vadim kozlovsky; 54–55(bg) Gunnar Pippel; 54(bc) Smileus, (cl) dslaven; 55(cl) Ray Hub; 56(cr) ifong; 56–57(bg) archibald; 58–59(bg) casejustin; 60–61(bg) Roman Chazov; 67(br) Lawrence Wee; 70–71(bg) Nerthuz; 72–73(bg) Petrosg; 75(tr) beerkoff; 76–77(bg) Bella D; 77(cl) Paul Matthew Photography; 79(tl) Elena Elisseeva; 80(bl) Bobbie Sandlin; 81(tr) dell; 83(tr) Patricia Marroquin, (bl) Yakobchuk Viacheslav; 84–85(bg) George Burba; 90(bg) Michael Rosskothen; 91(bg) Marilyn Volan; 92(*Spinosaurus*) Kostiantyn Ivanyshen, (*Giganotosaurus*) Linda Bucklin, (*T rex*) DM7, (*Allosaurus*) Jean-Michel Girard; 96–97(bg) Igor Janicek; 98(crab) Richard Waters, (bird) Steve Byland; 99(br) Rita Januskeviciute; 100(tr) Pan Xunbin, (bl) Wim Claes; 101(tr) Van Kuzmin; 103(br) Cathy Keifer; 105(bl) Incredible Arctic, (tr) BMJ; 106(bg) Targn Pleiades, (l) Florian Andronache, (cl) & (cr) Eduardo Rivero, (r) Clinton Moffat, (bg) BMJ; 108–109(bg) Eric Isselee; 109(tr) aaltair; 110(bc) cbpix; 112(br) Volkov Alexey; 113(bg) Tan Hung Meng; 118(bg) diversepixel; 119(bg) hameleonsEye; 122(bg) diversepixel; 124(bg) mountainpix; 128(cl) Tancha; 129(bg) Matsumoto; 130(b) MysticaLink; 130–131(bg) Evannovostro; 131(cl) Vladimir Korostyshevskiy;

ACKNOWLEDGEMENTS

137(bg) Federico Rostagno; 138–139(bg) Elenamiv; 143(bl) Kpa/Zuma/Rex; 144(tl) Konstanttin; 144–145(bg) Vitaly Korovin; 145(tc) Apostrophe, (b) Filip Fuxa; 146–147(bg) Luba V Nel; 148(t) jbstock, (bg) mg1408; 149(tr) Viacheslav Lopatin; 150(tl) & 151(br) Vitaly Korovin; 151(tr) ESB Professional, (bl) & (cr) Valentin Agapov; 152(tl) paper Piotr Zajc, (bg) blue paper Vitaly Korovin; 153(bl) paper Konstanttin, (tr) paper Molodec, (l) coin Paul Picone, (bc) coin I.Pilon, (r) coin Chris Hill; 154(tl) Konstanttin, (bl) Piotr Zajc; 155(tl) Lora liu

Superstock 147(cl) Christian Handl/imageBROKER; 152(tc) Universal Images Group; 155(tr) DeAgostini

Topfoto 26(bg) CM Dixon/HIP; 131(tr) Tom Hanley; 153(bl) Granger, NYC

All other photographs are from:
Digital Stock, digitalvision, ImageState, John Foxx, PhotoAlto, PhotoDisc, PhotoEssentials, PhotoPro, Stockbyte

Every effort has been made to acknowledge the source and copyright holder of each picture.
Miles Kelly Publishing apologizes for any unintentional errors or omissions.